4. Let there be light

Try using your water bottle as an improvised lantern: tie a headlamp to the bottle with the light shining inwards and use it to find your way round the campsite in the dark.

5. Great cinema

Turn simple foil into a popcorn machine in just a few steps: cut the foil into large squares, add 1 tbsp oil and 1 tbsp popcorn kernels and fold each one up into a pouch. Slide each foil package onto a stick and hold it over the campfire, shaking it every so often, until the corn starts popping. Open the foil carefully, add a blob of butter, and some salt or sugar as desired. The popcorn is ready!

6. Natural mosquito repellent

For us, the scent of rosemary and sage is reminiscent of a typical Mediterranean holiday, but these herbs have an added bonus because mosquitos can't stand the smell of them. If you burn these herbs on the campfire, they will emit an odour that should keep the little beasties away. Does it work? Well it's a popular household remedy, so it's got to be worth a try.

THE CAMPFIRE
COOKBOOK

THE CAMPFIRE COOKBOOK

80 IMAGINATIVE RECIPES FOR COOKING OUTDOORS

Viola Lex
Nico Stanitzok

7 Preface

8 Which type of camper are you?

There are many different types of camper, but which one are you? A free spirit in a retro camper van, a deluxe glamping type, or a family or festival camper?

10 Enjoy your holiday!

Check this guide to the camping kitchen and the key to the symbols used throughout the book so you can relax and enjoy your scaled-down kitchen.

12 The mobile store cupboard

Convenience is key when it comes to your mobile store cupboard. Find space-saving solutions for kitchen essentials and try recipes for Banana ketchup, Bircher muesli, and Dukkah spice mix – all useful additions to your luggage.

22 On the road

Motorway service food is best left by the wayside. Instead try making portable snacks, such as Poppy seed crackers with sesame, Mini meatball skewers, Layered salad in a jar, or Italian-style sandwiches with tomato and tahini, to fuel on your journey.

48 Keep it local

Track down regional specialities at local markets so you can be creative with your cooking, and follow advice on how to keep fresh food nice and cool so it stays fresh. Try making our Orange and avocado salad, Strawberry salad with mozzarella, or Country potato salad.

66 Cooking outdoors – a great experience!

Cooking on a camping stove is part of the whole outdoor adventure. Whether you have one or two burners, you can easily rustle up our Fettuccine "Alfredo", Croque Madame, Bread rolls from a pan, or Pan-cooked apple cake.

88–91 Born to be wild

True nature lovers are happiest right out in the wilderness where they can cook under a canopy of stars.

112 Fire it up

It's time to get grilling: if you fancy filled steaks, barbecue pizza, hot dogs wrapped in bacon, prawn and lime kebabs, barbecued sea bass, or chocolate cake baked in the embers, cooking over a fire or barbecue gives you that fresh-from-the-grill feeling.

134–135 Crazy about campfires?

Try our campfire bread recipes. Sitting around the fire waiting for bread to cook helps to set spirits soaring.

156 Extras

Check the ingredient packing list for vital food supplies and the equipment packing list for basic kit and luxury items.

158 Index

160 Acknowledgments

Off on new adventures!

If it's the sense of independence in particular that attracts you to camping, we know exactly how you feel. Camping is like a fusion of wanderlust and joie de vivre. It is pure freedom!

We like to think of ourselves as globetrotters, always on the move, trying to quench our insatiable desire to travel. It's a passion we share and that inspired us to create this cookbook. Travel has brought us such joy and we want you to experience some of that, too. We'd like to accompany you on your journey with our book – full of useful tips and fine food.

We know from our own experiences that cooking outdoors has far more to offer than packet soup and tinned ravioli. We have happy memories of childhood days at various camp sites and also recall more daring exploits as adults. I, Nico, am at my most content when immersed in the natural world, and for Viola, bliss is a VW camper van (a T3 with the nickname "Lucy", which belongs to her sister). As backpackers, we've already trekked all over the globe. Viola has pitched her tent in the Colombian jungle and at one point my desire for adventure grew so strong that I went off to live in Thailand.

All the things that really excite us about camping are here in this book. It's the ideal guide for your camping trip: it doesn't matter whether you are a large family or a solo festival-goer, young or old, thrifty or spendthrift – the main thing is, you need to be hungry for the outside life!

We hope you really enjoy our camping cookbook.

Viola Lex & Nico Stanitzok

Which type of camper are you?

The camper van enthusiast

Free spirits feel totally at home in a retro camper van and you will often see stylish surfing types travelling in them! A popular trip with camper van users is to potter leisurely cross-country around Australia or New Zealand. Here's a typical schedule for a camper van enthusiast: have a lie in, do a yoga session, go surfing, grab some rays, enjoy a beer.

The luxury camper

These campers don't like to be without their creature comforts on holiday, so they transform their mega-caravans into luxury oases on wheels, complete with a high-tech kitchen, washing machine, flat-screen TV, and even a garage – everything is on board! Or some prefer "glamping", which is currently all the rage, with camping accommodation provided in well-equipped and partially furnished luxury tents at glamorous sites.

The wild camper

"Back to your roots" is the motto for the inveterate wild camper. These genuine nature lovers are eager for adventure and like to hike, cook over a camp fire, and camp out in the wilderness. Equipment – from underwear through to cooking utensils – has to be functional for this kind of camper.

The family camper

Whether in a caravan or a tent, these campers are determined to take everything but the kitchen sink with them on their travels. Bicycles, wind breakers – you name it, you'll find it in their luggage. The "new parent" camper is also often seen on campsites. Newbie mums and dads are big fans of mobile accommodation for their first holiday with the baby.

The festival camper

Festival goers want one thing above all else: a party! A place to sleep merely serves as somewhere to chill out briefly between all the dancing. For these kinds of campers, everything needs to be uncomplicated and practical. After all, who wants to waste time setting up camp or cooking when you'd rather be partying?

The long-term camper

The long-term camper can be thought of as the campsite's indigenous inhabitant. These campers laboriously transform their plot into a second home, complete with tent and awning, kitchenette, and TV connection. They are both mocked and feared, but there's no need to be frightened of these unofficial "bosses": new arrivals are usually warmly welcomed by them.

Enjoy your holiday!

Once you've filled up the tank in the camper van or have got the tent ready for action, your trip can begin. You can call anywhere in the world home and decide on the spur of the moment where to spend the night. Relaxation is the order of the day! Travelling this way is addictive – and it works up an appetite! Despite having only a small kitchen, there's no need to miss out when you're camping – especially when it comes to the pleasure of eating, as we will reveal!

A camping trip requires good preparation, which is why even the most relaxed outdoor adventurers suddenly become avid list writers. However, there's no need to start fretting because we've taken charge of the planning so you can relax and simply pack. You'll find check lists for basic ingredients and kitchen equipment on p156. To make your life even easier, we have also provided great ideas for supplies on p12, camping stove tips on p66, and clever skills for the barbecue on p112 – as well as lots of other survival tips for campers.

Relax

Holidays often start in the local supermarket where you can saunter round the aisles and discover what your holiday destination has to offer. Our cookbook is full of recipes to inspire you and help you enjoy the feeling of eating outdoors, in the fresh air, together and happy! Even if you have only a small camping kitchen, our recipes are guaranteed to succeed. They are amazingly delicious and easy to follow – from one-pot dishes to pan-cooked bread. Et voilà... the food is ready!

Camping kitchen secrets

The aim is to keep things simple, so anything you don't need should be left at home, such as the kitchen scales. For our recipes you need only a tablespoon, teaspoon, or cup or favourite camping mug with a capacity of 250ml (9fl oz) for measuring. Where other measures are given, simply purchase the amount needed or use the measures on packaging to guide you on amounts. What else needs to be packed? This book of course. We've had it made in a handy format for travelling so you'll always have plenty of camping recipes up your sleeve during your travels.

Get cooking

It doesn't matter if you are a solo camper, a couple, or a four-person family – to make sure everyone gets their fill, we've designed the recipes to feed four people. The only exception is if you are cooking with just one camping stove burner or if you're preparing one of our instant dishes, in which case the ingredients will be enough for two people. If you do end up with leftovers, you can look forward to finishing these off the following day. But wait and see – camping usually makes you very hungry, and you might have a spontaneous visit from your camping neighbours!

Useful symbols

The following symbols are used throughout the book to help you choose the most suitable recipes:

 Road trip: Prepare these recipes before you set off. They are great for the outbound journey or for trips while away.

 Cold dishes: These can be made without a gas stove or a barbecue.

 Gas stove with 1 burner: You need a single saucepan or frying pan only for these dishes.

 Gas stove with 2 burners: You will need to use two pans at the same time for these dishes.

 Barbecue: These recipes are prepared on the barbecue.

 Tips and information: Includes clever tips for recipes or general advice for campers.

All in the timing

We cook our recipes using a camping stove or barbecue, but every camper has their own personal preference, so our recipes also work with other types of equipment. It doesn't matter what equipment you choose, just remember that cooking times will vary. Factors that can affect cooking time include the specific equipment and fuel used as well as the temperature. The recipes in this book give approximate timings, so use these as a guideline only. Always test to make sure your food is cooked.

The mobile store cupboard

Space-saving solutions

Make sure your holiday time is dedicated to enjoying the finer things in life, not on wasting time hunting for basic ingredients. Before you set off, decant pasta and flour into rectangular storage containers, which are ideal for stacking when space is at a premium. You can also pack up sugar, stock, washing up liquid, and special ingredients such as capers in handy travel containers.

Camping kitchen essentials

If you want to travel with minimal luggage, you'll love these lightweight items. Resealable freezer bags are super versatile for outdoor cooking and eating. They can be used to store ready-made muesli mixtures for breakfast, power snacks for when you're on the move, marinades for meat, or portions of "instant" meals that just need rehydrating (see recipes, pp90–91). And when you're camping you can't be without foil – an essential item.

Spice combos

Whether it's rosemary, cinnamon, or paprika, spices and herbs are crucial in a campsite kitchen. You can either buy spice boxes that can accommodate lots of little portions of different herbs or spice combinations, or just decant your favourites into empty containers – and don't forget to label them! Then you can enjoy discovering fresh herbs at local markets. And if you are really confident about identifying plants, you could collect wild herbs – where permitted.

Home-made condiments

Home-made food can't be beaten when it comes to taste – and the same is true for delicious home-made barbecue sauces. There's no need to dispense with the do-it-yourself trend for supplies when travelling. Clever campers prepare ketchup and barbecue sauces (see recipes, pp14–16) in their kitchen at home then take these along with them.

All-rounders

It's worth planning your supplies well so that one ingredient can be used for several recipes. Pack some cocoa powder and use it to make Pan-cooked apple cake (see p110) or Chocolate cake (see p155) plus hot chocolate every morning for the kids. The same applies when shopping locally: for example, put a double portion of feta cheese into your shopping basket so you can cook Green asparagus salad (see p54) for lunch followed by Greek pan-cooked pasta (see p80) for supper.

Thirst quenchers

Before you leave, freeze plastic bottles filled with still water. This is a double bonus because you'll have drinking water on hand for the journey, plus while the bottles are defrosting in the cool box, any food stored alongside them will be kept cold. Remember, though, water expands when it freezes. Tip a generous splash of water out of the bottle before freezing.

Ketchup

2 tbsp rapeseed oil
2 onions, diced
5 tbsp sugar
4 tbsp cider vinegar
2 tbsp apple purée
2 x 400g cans chopped tomatoes
½ tsp curry powder
salt

Also

2 screw-top bottles (500ml/16fl oz
 each), rinsed with hot water

1 Heat the oil in a pan. Sweat the onions in the hot oil over a moderate heat for 2 minutes. Add the sugar and sauté over a low heat for a further 6 minutes.

2 Add the vinegar to deglaze the pan, then add the apple purée, tomatoes, and curry powder, stir, and simmer over a moderate heat for about 10 minutes, stirring occasionally to prevent the sauce from sticking to the pan. Finally, purée the mixture using a hand-held blender and season to taste with salt. Decant into bottles through a funnel while it is still hot then seal. The sealed ketchup will keep unrefrigerated for up to a month. Once opened, refrigerate and use within 2 weeks.

Banana ketchup

2 tbsp groundnut oil
1 small onion, diced
2 garlic cloves, finely chopped or crushed
1 jalapeño chilli, deseeded and halved
4cm (1¾in) piece of ginger, peeled and
  grated
½ tsp ground turmeric
¼ tsp ground allspice
100ml (3½fl oz) white wine vinegar
2 tbsp honey
2 tbsp dark rum
1 tbsp tomato purée
1 tbsp soy sauce
4 bananas
salt

Also

2 screw-top bottles (500ml/16fl oz each),
  rinsed with hot water

1 Heat the oil in a pan. Sweat the onion over a moderate heat for 5 minutes. Add the garlic, chilli, ginger, turmeric, and allspice and sauté for 30 seconds. Add the vinegar to deglaze the pan, then add the honey, rum, tomato purée, and soy sauce and stir until smooth. Peel the bananas, chop into rough pieces, and add to the pan. Cover with a lid and simmer over a low heat for 15 minutes, stirring regularly. Remove the pan from the hob and leave to cool for 10 minutes.

2 Transfer the banana mixture to a food processor and purée well for about 1 minute, adding water as needed to produce the desired consistency. Alternatively, purée the mixture using a hand-held blender.

3 Return the mixture to the pan and bring to the boil once more, stirring constantly. Season to taste with salt. Transfer into bottles while boiling hot and seal immediately. The sealed ketchup will keep unrefrigerated for up to a month. Once opened, refrigerate and use within 2 weeks.

Family holiday trial run
If you're planning a family camping trip but your kids have never spent a night in a tent before, give them a trial run before you head off into the distance on your annual holiday. Go on a short weekend camping trip together first or simply pitch your tent in the garden for a night.

BBQ sauce

1 tbsp rapeseed oil
2 onions, diced
1 red pepper, deseeded and diced
2 red chillies, deseeded and quartered
400g can peeled tomatoes
½ cup honey
1 tsp smoked salt, plus extra, to taste,
   and freshly ground black pepper
2 tbsp balsamic vinegar
1 tsp cornflour

Also

2 screw-top bottles (300ml/10fl oz
   each), rinsed with hot water

1 Heat the oil in a pan. Sweat the onions, pepper, and chillies over a
moderate heat for 5 minutes. Add the tomatoes, honey, and salt.
Combine the vinegar and cornflour and stir into the mixture with a
balloon whisk. Simmer everything for 10 minutes over a moderate heat,
stirring occasionally.

2 Purée the thickened BBQ sauce with a hand-held blender and season
to taste with salt and pepper. Decant into the bottles while still hot,
and seal. The sealed BBQ sauce will keep unrefrigerated for a month.
Once opened, refrigerate and use within 2 weeks.

Smoked sophistication

Smoked salt is an aromatic salt that imbues dishes with a
wonderful smoky flavour. This is a strong seasoning with an
intense flavour, so be sparing when you first add it and taste
everything again at the end.

For about 8 steaks or 2-3 flatbreads · preparation time about 20 minutes

Dukkah – Middle-Eastern or African spice mixture

2 dried chillies
50g (1¾oz) roasted, salted peanuts, finely chopped
50g (1¾oz) hazelnuts, finely chopped
50g (1¾oz) pistachios, finely chopped
20g (¾oz) sesame seeds
3 tsp garlic granules
2 tsp ground cumin
2 tsp ground coriander
5 tsp fennel seeds
3 tsp coarse salt

1 Crush the chilli in a mortar or shred it with your fingers. Toast the nuts, chillies, sesame seeds, garlic, spices, and salt in a dry pan over a moderate heat until they release their aroma.

2 Leave to cool then transfer to a freezer bag or screw-top jar to take with you on your trip.

Tastes fantastic with...
Try this mix with freshly baked flatbreads, dipped into olive oil and then into the dukkah mixture. Or toss some fish in dukkah before serving – we guarantee you'll experience aromatic pyrotechnics!

Makes 4 portions
Preparation time about 20 minutes · baking time 35-40 minutes

Apricot cakes in a jar

4 tbsp white breadcrumbs
1½ cups dried apricots, finely
 diced
1½ cups plain flour, plus 1 tbsp
250g (9oz) soft butter
1 cup sugar
juice of 2 oranges (about ½ cup)
 and zest of 1 orange
2-3 drops vanilla extract
4 eggs
½ cup cornflour
2 tsp baking powder

Also
4 preserving jars with lids
 (500ml/16fl oz each)

1 Grease the jars and scatter 1 tablespoon of white breadcrumbs
 into each. Make sure that the glass rim, which will later be in
contact with the rubber seal, is left clear. Preheat the oven to 180°C
(350°F/Gas 4). Combine the apricots and with the 1 tablespoon of
flour in a bowl.

2 Cream the butter with the sugar and the orange zest using an
 electric hand-held blender, add the vanilla extract, then gradually
stir in the eggs one at a time, mixing for 30 seconds after each
addition. Combine the 1½ cups of flour, cornflour, and baking
powder and add to the mix with the orange juice. Stir until combined,
then fold in the apricots.

3 Divide the mixture between the jars so they are about two-thirds
 full. Place in the centre of the oven and bake for 35-40 minutes.
Meanwhile, soak 4 rubber seals for the jars in water.

4 Remove the jars from the oven and place the rubber rings on the
 rim. Seal immediately with the lids and clip in place with the
clasp. Leave the cakes to cool on a rack in the sealed jars. They will
keep for about 2 weeks unopened and unrefrigerated. Tip them out
of the jars to serve.

 For 4 people or to store · preparation time about 10 minutes + soaking overnight

Camping Bircher muesli mixture

2 cups jumbo oats
4 tbsp hazelnuts, chopped
juice of 1 orange
100ml (3½fl oz) milk
200g (7oz) low-fat fromage frais
300g (10oz) low-fat yogurt
2 tbsp honey
1 apple, finely diced or roughly grated

1 Combine the oats and hazelnuts in a bowl at home. Transfer to a small screw-top jar or freezer bag, seal and take this with you, ready-prepared, on your trip.

2 Take the fromage frais out of the fridge 20 minutes before using to soften it. Stir the orange juice and milk together in a bowl. Add the fromage frais, yogurt, and honey and stir everything until smoothly combined. Stir in the muesli mixture and leave to soak overnight. Before serving, fold the apple into the muesli then divide the muesli between 4 bowls and serve.

Cranberry muesli bars

1 cup dried cranberries
4 tbsp butter
3 tbsp sugar
2 tbsp honey
1 tsp lemon juice
2 cups jumbo oats
⅓ cup chopped almonds
2 tbsp sunflower seeds

Also
baking parchment
baking dish (roughly 20 × 30cm/8 x 12in)

1 Line the ovenproof dish with the baking parchment and preheat the oven to 160°C (325°F/Gas 3). Finely chop the cranberries with a knife or blitz them in the food processor.

2 Place the butter, sugar, honey, and lemon juice in a small pan and stir over a moderate heat until the sugar has completely dissolved. Combine the cranberries, oats, almonds, and sunflower seeds in a bowl. Carefully stir in the butter mixture, making sure everything is coated.

3 Transfer the mixture to the ovenproof dish, smooth the surface, and press it down slightly. Bake in the centre of the oven for about 20 minutes.

4 Remove and leave to cool in the dish. Use the parchment paper to lift it out of the dish, then slice into 12 bars.

On the road

Take it along with you

If you're eager to hit the road, but find that typical service station food is best avoided, just rustle up a couple of "snacks to go" while you're still at home (see recipes from p24). Our sandwiches are also ideal for day trips once you're at your holiday destination – whether you're off hiking in the mountains or enjoying a relaxing day at the beach.

Refuelling

Do you need a quick burst of energy? Our supplies for the journey are perfect for a power break. While your holiday preparations are underway, get your oven working overtime to prepare roasted Honey-roasted peanuts (see p30) or Cranberry muesli bars (see p21). These pick-me-up snacks will fit easily into your rucksack in resealable freezer bags.

Pop it in a bag

Anyone who has ever eaten a sandwich on a car journey will recognize the scenario: no sooner do you take a bite from your roll than the tomato falls out onto the seat and the sauce is in your lap. To prevent this, pack up your sandwiches in paper bags: reused snack bags made from paper (such as kebab wrappers) are a neat solution.

Shake it up

Using "salad shakers" makes life easier when you're on the move. These containers place the salad ingredients in a screw-top container and the dressing in a separate container in the lid, so the salad stays crisp and fresh. When you want to eat, just mix it all together. Shake it up!

A tight squeeze

Take a reusable drinking bottle with you on your journey. If you are scrambling for every last millimetre of space and watching every gram of weight, it's worth acquiring a squashable drinking bottle, which can be squeezed smaller when empty. And for anyone who is prone to getting cold feet: pour hot water into the bottle, wrap a t-shirt round it, and place it in your sleeping bag – hey presto, you have a home-made hot-water bottle.

Simple crackers

2 cups plain flour, plus extra
  for dusting
3 tsp baking powder
1 tbsp sugar
1 tsp salt
8 tbsp chilled butter
2 tbsp rapeseed oil

Also
baking parchment
biscuit cutters

1 Line 2 baking trays with baking parchment. Preheat the oven to 200°C (400°F/Gas 6). Put the flour, baking powder, sugar, and ½ teaspoon of the salt in a bowl and mix well. Chop 80g (2¾oz) of the butter into pieces and add to the bowl. Knead everything together quickly with your hands. Add the oil and work into the mixture. Gradually add 3½ tablespoons of cold water and knead in to a smooth dough.

2 Roll out the dough on a floured work surface to about 3mm (⅛in) thick. Stamp out cracker shapes and place on the baking trays. Prick each cracker with a fork. Slide the trays into the centre of the oven and bake the crackers for 12–14 minutes, until golden brown.

3 Melt the remaining butter and combine with the remaining salt. Remove the crackers from the oven and leave to cool. Brush with the melted salted butter while still hot.

Makes about 100 pieces · preparation time about 1 hour · baking time about 12 minutes

Poppy seed crackers with sesame

2½ cups plain flour, plus extra for
  dusting
2 tbsp olive oil
salt
2 tbsp poppy seeds
1 tbsp sesame seeds
2 tbsp coarse sea salt

Also
cling film
baking parchment

1 Use your hands to combine 1½ cups of the flour with 150ml (5fl oz)
water, the olive oil, and a pinch of salt in a bowl. Add the remaining
flour and the poppy and sesame seeds and knead everything by hand until
you have a smooth dough. Wrap in cling film and rest for 30 minutes.

2 Meanwhile, line 2 baking trays with baking parchment. Preheat the
oven to 220°C (425°F/Gas 7). Roll out the dough on a floured work
surface to about 5mm (¼in) thick. Slice into 3cm (1½in) squares with a
pastry wheel. Place the crackers on the baking trays. Scatter with sea salt.

3 Put the trays in the centre of the oven and bake the crackers for
12–15 minutes, until golden brown. Take the trays out of the oven, use
the paper to remove the crackers, and leave them to cool on a wire rack.

Mini meatball skewers

For the meatballs
½ bread roll
1 red onion, finely sliced
½ bunch of flat-leaf parsley, finely chopped
500g (1lb 2oz) minced meat
1 egg
1 tbsp white breadcrumbs
1 tsp medium–hot mustard
1 tsp sweet paprika
1 tsp curry powder
salt and freshly ground black pepper
2 tbsp rapeseed oil
16 cherry tomatoes
Gouda cheese, cut into 8 bite-sized cubes

Also
8 wooden skewers (15cm/6in each)

1 Soak the bread in hot water. Squeeze out the roll and place in a bowl with the onion, parsley, minced meat, egg, white breadcrumbs, mustard, paprika, and curry powder. Knead everything thoroughly with your hands until the mixture is well combined. Season to taste with salt and pepper and leave to rest for 10 minutes.

2 Shape 24 evenly sized balls from the meat mixture. Heat the oil in a pan. Fry the meatballs over a moderate heat for about 10 minutes until golden brown all over. Remove and drain on some kitchen paper and leave to cool completely.

3 Meanwhile, wash the cherry tomatoes and leave to drain. Slide 3 meatballs, 2 tomatoes, and a piece of cheese onto each skewer. Pack up into paper bags or put in an airtight container for the trip.

Two in one
Salt and pepper are crucial when cooking. For your camping kitchen, a functional piece of equipment for this spice duo is a dispenser that screws together from two sides so that each side can be filled with the separate condiments.

For 4 people
Preparation time about 20 minutes · infusion time about 24 hours

Layered salad in a jar

285g can sweetcorn
235g can pineapple pieces
3 celery sticks
2 eggs
3 tbsp mayonnaise
200g (7oz) low-fat yogurt
salt and freshly ground black pepper
1 small leek, halved lengthways, then cut
   into 3mm (⅛in) strips
¼ iceberg lettuce, thinly sliced
150g (5½oz) Gouda, sliced into
   5mm (¼in) strips
150g (5½oz) cooked ham, sliced into
   5mm (¼in) strips

Also
4 screw-top jars (400ml/14fl oz each)

1 Strain the sweetcorn, pineapple, and celery in a sieve and leave to drain. Cook the eggs in boiling water for 8 minutes then plunge them into cold water, peel, and leave to cool.

2 Combine the mayonnaise and yogurt in a bowl and season to taste with salt and pepper.

3 Layer up all the ingredients except the cheese and eggs so they are evenly distributed in the jars and drizzle with the mayonnaise dressing. Scatter over the cheese as the final layer. Chop the eggs into quarters and distribute between the jars. Seal the jars with the lids and leave the salad in the fridge to infuse for about 24 hours.

Honey-roasted peanuts

500g (1lb 2oz) roasted, unsalted peanuts
1 cup honey
1 cup sugar
2 tsp salt

Also
baking parchment

1 Line a baking tray with baking parchment. Preheat the oven to 170°C (350°F/Gas 3½). Put the peanuts in a bowl. Heat the honey in a pan over a moderate heat until runny then pour the honey over the peanuts. Add the sugar and salt and stir everything well until the peanuts are completely coated in honey and sugar.

2 Spread the peanuts evenly over the baking tray, trying to ensure they aren't touching.

3 Slide the tray into the centre of the oven and roast for about 15 minutes, turning the nuts half-way through. When the nuts are golden, remove and leave to cool completely on the tray.

4 Break up the nut mixture with your fingers and transfer to an airtight container, or to a paper bag or freezer bag, ready for your hike or journey.

Papaya, banana, and nut mix

5 tbsp banana chips
4 tbsp dried papaya, finely chopped
2 tbsp dried pineapple, finely
  chopped
1 cup whole almonds
1 cup cashews
5 tbsp pumpkin seeds
5 tbsp puffed quinoa
3 tbsp coconut flakes

1 Break the banana chips into small pieces. Mix all the ingredients in a bowl then decant into an airtight box. The nut mixture can also be transferred to a paper or freezer bag for your journey.

Old school

Remember the days before sat nav and Google Maps? Even if it feels like taking a trip back in time, it's always advisable to take a trusty old road map with you. If your sat nav or smartphone fail, the map will never let you down. Not to mention it's fun navigating yourself every now and then!

For 4 people · preparation time about 15 minutes · baking time about 30 minutes

Spiced nuts with pecorino

2 cups roasted, unsalted pistachios,
  shells removed
1 cup whole almonds
2 cups walnuts
1 cup hazelnuts
2 tbsp honey
3 tbsp raw cane sugar
1 tsp smoked paprika
1 tsp ground cumin
½ tsp chilli flakes
pinch of ground cinnamon
200g (7oz) Pecorino cheese

Also
baking parchment

1 Mix together the pistachios, almonds, walnuts, and hazelnuts. Line a baking tray with baking parchment. Preheat the oven to 150°C (300°F/Gas 2). Put the honey and sugar into a pan and bring to the boil over a moderate heat, stirring constantly. Once the sugar has dissolved, reduce the temperature and let the mixture simmer over a low heat for another minute. Stir in the spices, add the nuts, and stir again until everything is covered with the honey mixture.

2 Spread the nuts evenly over the baking tray, trying to ensure they aren't touching. Slide the tray into the centre of the oven and roast the nuts for 30 minutes. Turn them every 10 minutes then remove from the oven and leave to cool completely on the tray.

3 Roughly grate the cheese. Break apart the nut mixture, combine with the cheese, and transfer to an airtight container.

For 4 people
Preparation time about 15 minutes · resting time 30 minutes

Mini sandwich rolls with creamed tuna

150g can tuna
1 small onion, diced
3 tbsp mayonnaise
½ tsp dried basil
salt and freshly ground black pepper
8 slices of white sliced bread, crusts
  removed
¼ cucumber, peeled and quartered
  lengthways

Also
2 pieces of cling film (30 × 50cm/
  12 x 20in)

1 Drain the tuna in a sieve. Put the drained tuna, onion, mayonnaise, and basil into a blender beaker and purée well using a hand-held blender (see also tip, below). Season to taste with salt and pepper.

2 Roll out the slices of bread on the work surface with a rolling pin until they are as flat as possible. Spread the cling film on a separate part of the work surface and place 2 slices of bread next to each other on it, so they overlap in the middle by about 1cm (½in). Spread the tuna mixture evenly over the slices of bread. Place 2 strips of cucumber on the lower edge of each one and use the cling film to help you roll up the slices of bread as tightly as possible. Repeat with the rest of the slices. Chill for about 30 minutes, then unwrap and slice into 2–3cm (¾–1½in) thick rounds.

On a knife-edge
If you are preparing this recipe at home for your journey, you'll probably use a blender. In an improvised campsite kitchen, just chop everything very finely with a knife instead. Depending on the recipe you are preparing, if you have to manage without a blender, you can either press the ingredients using a fork, or push them through a sieve.

For 4 people
Preparation time about 20 minutes

Crispy baguette with turkey and apricots

8 very thin turkey breast steaks (50g/1¾oz each, or 4 x 100g/3½oz steaks), pounded flat
salt and freshly ground black pepper
1 tbsp rapeseed oil
8 slices bacon
1 cup soft apricots, finely chopped
3cm (1½in) piece of ginger, grated
1 red chilli, deseeded and finely chopped
2 tbsp honey
1 tsp mustard
1 tbsp white wine vinegar
4 tbsp mayonnaise
1 fresh baguette (about 50cm/20in long, 8cm/3¼in diameter)
6 radicchio leaves, cut into very thin strips

1 Season the turkey breast steaks with salt and pepper. Heat the oil in a pan and fry the steaks over a high heat for 1 minute on each side. Take them out of the pan, leave to drain on kitchen paper, and set aside. In the same pan, fry the bacon on both sides until golden brown and crisp, then set aside.

2 Stir the apricots, ginger, chilli, honey, mustard, vinegar, and mayonnaise together in a bowl and season to taste with salt and pepper.

3 Slice the baguette lengthways. Spread the apricot mayonnaise evenly over the surface. Scatter over the radicchio. First add the bacon, then the turkey breast to the baguette. Fold it shut, press firmly, and slice into 4 equal-sized sections. Serve immediately, or wrap up in greaseproof paper for your trip.

That certain something
Toast the filled baguette on a grill for about 1 minute each side to make it even more delicious. The turkey breast and bacon can also be prepared on the barbecue or grill.

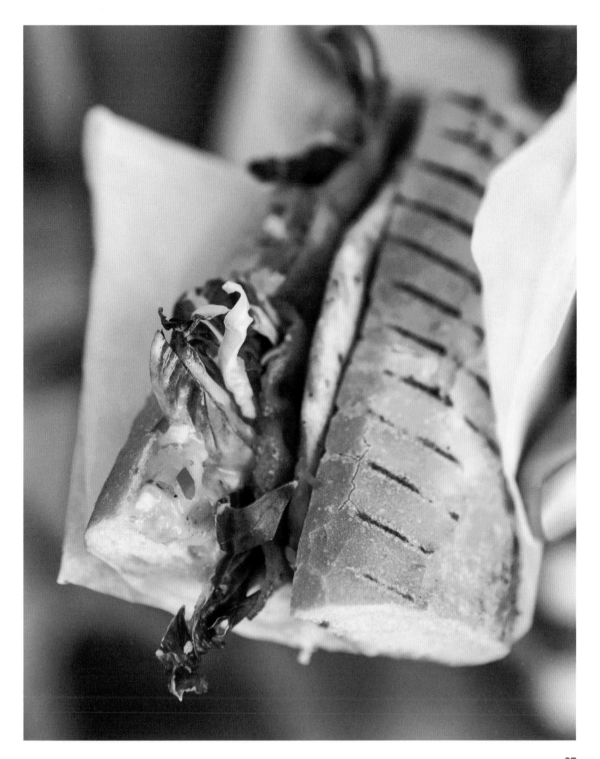

For 4 people
Preparation time about 20 minutes

Sandwiches with ricotta and figs

200g (7oz) ricotta
1 tbsp olive oil
3cm (1½in) piece ginger, peeled and
  finely chopped
1 garlic clove, finely chopped or crushed
¼ tsp chilli flakes
¼ tsp dried oregano
pinch of grated nutmeg
salt and freshly ground black pepper
4–5 sundried tomatoes (in oil), finely diced
8 slices of white bread
8 thin slices of Parma ham
3 figs, thinly sliced

1 Put the ricotta into a bowl and stir in the oil. Season with the ginger, garlic, chilli flakes, oregano, nutmeg, and salt and pepper. Add the sundried tomatoes.

2 Spread the mixture over the bread and place a slice of Parma ham on top of each one, then lay the fig slices on the ham. Place the bread slices with filled sides together and press firmly.

3 Toast the sandwiches on a grill over a moderate heat on both sides until golden brown. Alternatively, they can also be prepared on the hob or a camping stove. To do this, heat 2 tablespoons of olive oil in a pan and fry the sandwiches over a moderate heat on both sides until golden brown. Remove from the pan, slice the filled bread in half diagonally, and serve straight away – or enjoy them cold on the road.

For 4 people
Preparation time about 10 minutes

Strawberry sandwich

4 tbsp chocolate hazelnut spread
8 slices of white bread
100g (3½oz) strawberries, cut into
   3mm (⅛in) thick slices
8 marshmallows, cut into 5mm (¼in)
   thick slices
3 tbsp ground almonds

1 Spread the chocolate hazelnut spread evenly over 4 slices of the
bread. Place the sliced strawberries in a layer on top and cover
these with the sliced marshmallows.

2 Scatter over the almonds and top with the remaining slices of
bread. Press together firmly and slice in half diagonally to serve.

Hooray, there are marshmallows left over!
Slide leftover marshmallows onto wooden
skewers (soaked in water for at least 30 minutes
beforehand) and lay these on foil on the
barbecue. Or spear the marshmallows on a stick
and hold them over the campfire until they take
on a bit of colour. Wait a moment to let them cool
down – then tuck in!

For 4 people · preparation time about 20 minutes

Italian-style sandwiches with tahini and tomato

2 tbsp olive oil
3 beef tomatoes, cut into 1cm (½in)
 thick slices
salt and freshly ground black pepper
8 slices of white bread, crusts removed
1 garlic clove, halved
4 tbsp tahini (sesame seed paste)
2 tsp lemon juice
2 sprigs of mint leaves
pinch of dried oregano

1 Heat the oil in a pan. Sauté the tomato slices over a moderate heat and season with salt and pepper. In the meantime, toast the bread until crisp in a toaster or under the grill. Rub the garlic halves over the surface of the toasted slices of bread.

2 Stir the tahini into the lemon juice and season to taste with a bit of salt and pepper. Spread evenly over 4 slices of the bread and arrange the sliced tomato on top. Scatter the mint leaves over the tomatoes. Season with the oregano and top with the remaining 4 slices of bread. Slice diagonally and serve.

Italian-style sandwiches with ricotta and ham

4 tbsp ricotta
8 slices of white bread, crusts removed
100g (3½oz) prosciutto ham
2 tomatoes, cut into 3mm (⅛in) thick slices
1 tbsp balsamic vinegar
1 tbsp olive oil
salt and freshly ground black pepper
handful of rocket

1 Spread the slices of bread evenly with ricotta and top 4 of the slices with the ham.

2 Lay the tomatoes over the ham. Drizzle over a few drops of vinegar and oil and season generously with salt and pepper. Scatter the rocket over the tomatoes.

3 Place the 4 slices of bread with just ricotta cheese-side down on top of the tomato layer, pressing down firmly. Slice the sandwiches diagonally and serve.

For 4 people
Preparation time about 25 minutes

Ham and Cheddar wraps with honey-mustard sauce

2 tbsp full-fat yogurt
1 tbsp medium–hot mustard
2 tbsp honey
salt and freshly ground black pepper
8 slices of bacon
1 small romaine lettuce, halved lengthways
  and cut into thin strips
handful of rocket
2 tomatoes
4 large wheat tortillas
4 slices Cheddar
4 slices ham

1 To make the honey and mustard sauce, combine the yogurt, mustard, and honey in a bowl and season to taste with salt and pepper. Heat a pan without any oil. Place the bacon in the pan and fry over a moderate heat until crisp. Remove and leave to drain on kitchen paper.

2 Mix the lettuce with the rocket, wash, and leave to drain. Cut each tomato into 6 slices. Heat the tortillas one after another in a dry pan or on the grill over a moderate heat for 15 seconds each side.

3 Place a bit of lettuce and 3 slices of tomato in the centre of each tortilla and drizzle over 2 tablespoons of the sauce. Place 1 slice each of Cheddar and ham on the tomatoes and top with 2 rashers of bacon. Fold the short side of each tortilla over the filling, fold in the long side, and roll up the tortilla as tightly as possible before serving.

Extra tasty
The assembled wraps taste particularly good toasted until crispy. Do this either under the grill or heat them in a pan with a bit of butter. Absolutely delicious!

For 2 people
Preparation time about 15 minutes

Eggless pancakes

1¼ cups flour
1 tsp baking powder
3 tbsp sugar
½ tsp salt
200ml (7fl oz) milk
2–3 drops vanilla extract
5 tbsp rapeseed oil

Also
jam or hazelnut chocolate spread
(as desired)

1 Combine the flour, baking powder, sugar, and salt in a bowl. Stir in the milk (or alternatively use water or almond milk) and vanilla extract to create a smooth mixture.

2 Heat the oil in a pan. For each pancake, put 1 tablespoon of the mixture into the pan and cook over a moderate heat for about 1 minute on each side. Serve with jam or hazelnut chocolate spread.

Breakfast from a tube
Our pancake mixture is perfect for preparing ahead if you are able to chill it: decant into squeezy bottles, store in the fridge, and squirt portions directly into the pan. It's super easy, and will satisfy hungry campers in the morning in double-quick time.

Keep it local

Imagine it's early in the morning and you're setting off to the market. The sun is shining and there's plenty of hustle and bustle. Colourful stalls stand next to one another. On one stall you spot fragrant, sun-ripened tomatoes. Mmmm... you must grab some of those!

Whether it's French vegetables, Spanish sausage, Italian cheese, or German wine – regional shopping is an unforgettable experience. It's a pleasure for the senses and perfect for picking up fresh produce to add to your core supplies. Bear in mind, though, that some items need to be handled carefully and kept chilled throughout your trip.

Before you set off

There are a few basic supplies that are essential for a mobile store cupboard, such as spices, onions, garlic, oil, flour, and coffee (see packing list, p156). Also, canned items, such as tuna and beans, that don't need refrigerating and can be bought before leaving home, are highly practical. Then buy regional delicacies and fresh fruit and vegetables once you've reached your holiday destination.

Nice and cool

Dairy products (unless unopened UHT milk or almond milk), fish, and meat, which keep only for a short time, need to be stored at temperatures between 2°C and 6°C (36°F and 43°F). Keep these well chilled in airtight containers to protect them. You can judge whether something is still okay from its smell and appearance. Test before you eat: fresh foods have a neutral smell and meat and fish should be firm, resistant to pressure, and have a good colour. Since large quantities are difficult to accommodate in a tiny camping kitchen, it's best to shop frequently and use up food as quickly as possible.

Good to know: shelf life

Fresh fish: 1 day
Beef: 3 days
Veal and pork: 2 days
Poultry: 1–2 days
Minced meat: consume on day of purchase

From the cold store

A cool box with freezer blocks will suffice for keeping drinks cold, but the more often the box is opened, the faster the contents will warm. For ingredients such as sausages, cheese, meat, fish, or opened sauces, you will need a more effective, long-term solution. Electric cool boxes are available in various sizes and offer different operating modes.

When purchasing, consider how noisy the box is, whether it is suitable for longer trips, and check how reliably it will work at high external temperatures. Also find out the following: can the box be operated using a car battery (12 V), via the power supply system at the campsite (230 V), or with an energy-efficient solar system on the roof? If you want to keep all your options open, you will need to purchase a hybrid cooling device that can also run off gas, or you could just purchase a convenient camping fridge with a mini freezer compartment.

Stack them up

Stacking items is the best way to pack a cool box, ensuring that everything stays cool and dry.

1st layer (right at the bottom):
ideally lay a grill on the bottom so that nothing sits in water from condensation.

2nd layer:
keep frozen water bottles or freezer packs here, with food in rectangular storage containers packed in between.

3rd layer:
ideally place cheese, sausages, and grilled meat on another grill and then place additional cooling elements above this.

Ideally, eggs should be chilled (see also tip on p75).

For 4 people
Preparation time about 30 minutes

Orange and avocado salad with Dijon dressing

For the dressing

11 garlic cloves, finely chopped or crushed
2 tbsp mayonnaise
1 tbsp wholegrain Dijon mustard
2 tbsp honey
3 tbsp white wine vinegar
3 tbsp olive oil
1 tsp dried tarragon
salt and freshly ground black pepper

For the salad

5 oranges
1 pink grapefruit
1 blood orange
1 small fennel bulb, stalk removed then
   sliced into very thin strips or shredded
2 red onions, cut into thin strips
2 avocados, pitted and flesh diced
½ bunch of mint leaves

1 To make the dressing, add the garlic to the rest of the dressing ingredients in a bowl and combine with a balloon whisk until smooth. Season to taste with salt and pepper and set aside for now.

2 Cut off the peel and white pith of the oranges, grapefruit, and blood orange. Cut the fruit into roughly 5mm (¼in) thick slices and divide between the plates. Scatter the fennel over the citrus fruit.

3 Scatter the onions over the salad. Add the avocados and drizzle dressing evenly over everything. Garnish the salad with the mint leaves and serve.

For 4 people
Preparation time about 20 minutes · infusion time about 1 hour

Broccoli salad with cashews and Roquefort dressing

For the dressing

50g (1¾oz) Roquefort (or another blue
cheese)
1 garlic clove, finely chopped or crushed
3 tbsp white wine vinegar
1 tbsp lemon juice
1 tbsp sugar
pinch of cayenne
4 tbsp olive oil
2 tbsp full-fat yogurt

For the salad

1kg (2¼lb) broccoli, cut into small florets
2 sprigs of mint, stalks removed and leaves
roughly chopped
1 red onion, thinly sliced
50g (1¾oz) blueberries
2 tbsp sunflower seeds
4 tbsp cashews
salt and freshly ground black pepper

1 To make the dressing, finely crumble the Roquefort and add to a bowl with the garlic, vinegar, lemon juice, and sugar. Crush the Roquefort with a fork until it has almost completely dissolved. Put the remaining dressing ingredients into a large salad bowl and whisk until well combined using a balloon whisk. Then add the Roquefort mixture and combine.

2 Combine the broccoli, mint, onion, blueberries, sunflower seeds, and cashews. Drizzle over the dressing and mix everything carefully. Leave to stand for about 1 hour, then season to taste with salt and pepper before serving.

Eat it all!
Often broccoli stalks end up, needlessly, in the bin, even though they are perfect for making soup. Peel and finely chop 500g (1lb 2oz) broccoli stalk. Add to a pan with 250g (9oz) peeled and quartered potatoes and 750ml (1¼ pints) vegetable stock. Simmer for 25 minutes and purée with a hand-held blender. Add 100g (3½oz) cream and season with nutmeg and salt and pepper.

Green asparagus salad with feta cheese

For the salad
400g can kidney beans
600g (1lb 5oz) green asparagus
200g (7oz) green beans
2 carrots, peeled and grated
200g (7oz) feta cheese, cut into
   1cm (½in) cubes
bread rolls or flatbread, to serve

For the dressing
3 tbsp sherry vinegar
1 tbsp sugar
1 tsp dried oregano
1 tsp medium-hot mustard
4 tbsp olive oil
salt and freshly ground black pepper

1 Pour the kidney beans into a sieve, rinse, and leave to drain. Break off the woody end of the asparagus spears and peel the lower 3cm (1½in) of each spear. Slice the spears diagonally into 4–5cm (1¾–2in) long pieces. Slice the beans diagonally into roughly 3cm (1½in) long pieces.

2 Bring 1 litre (1¾ pints) salted water to the boil in a pan and cook the asparagus and beans for 6 minutes, until just tender. Drain, plunge into cold water, and leave to drain in a sieve.

3 Combine the grated carrot, diced cheese, kidney beans, asparagus, and green beans in a salad bowl.

4 Stir the dressing ingredients together in a bowl and season to taste with salt and pepper. Drizzle over the salad and arrange on 4 plates, then serve with fresh bread rolls or flatbread.

Tomato and sweetcorn salad with chickpeas

285g can sweetcorn
400g can chickpeas
1 garlic clove, finely chopped or
    crushed
3 tbsp mascarpone
3 tbsp white balsamic vinegar
2 tbsp honey
1 tbsp mayonnaise
½ bunch of basil, stalks removed and
    leaves chopped
salt and freshly ground black pepper
8 tomatoes, deseeded and quartered
8 radishes, halved
1 red onion, very finely sliced
3 spring onions

1 Strain the sweetcorn and chickpeas, rinse, then leave to drain. Add the garlic to a salad bowl with the mascarpone, vinegar, honey, and mayonnaise and stir until you have a smooth sauce. Add the chopped basil leaves to the salad dressing and season to taste with salt and pepper.

2 Chop the tomato quarters into 5mm (¼in) thick strips. Slice the radish halves into 3mm (⅛in) thick slices. Slice the spring onions into 5mm (¼in) wide rings. Add the onion, radishes, spring onions, sweetcorn, and chickpeas to the salad dressing, fold everything gently together, divide between 4 plates, and serve.

Strawberry salad with mozzarella

For the salad

2 tbsp butter

100g (3½oz) mie noodles, cut into 2cm (¾in) pieces

4 tbsp chopped almonds

3 tbsp sunflower seeds

2 handfuls of baby spinach, large leaves chopped

1 romaine lettuce, , stalk removed, quartered, then cut in 5mm (¼in) pieces

350g (12oz) strawberries, cut in 5mm (¼in) pieces

100g (3½oz) Parmesan shavings

200g (7oz) mini mozzarella balls

For the dressing

1 garlic clove, finely chopped or pressed

4 tbsp sugar

6 tbsp red wine vinegar

4 tbsp rapeseed oil

1 tsp paprika

salt and freshly ground black pepper

1 Melt the butter in a large pan and fry the noodles, almonds, and sunflower seeds over a moderate heat until golden brown. Remove from the hob and leave to cool.

2 Combine the spinach, lettuce, strawberries, Parmesan, and mozzarella in a salad bowl and set aside.

3 To make the dressing, mix the garlic, sugar, and vinegar together in a bowl until the sugar has dissolved. Stir in the oil and paprika and season to taste with salt and pepper. Mix the salad with the dressing and divide between 4 plates. Scatter over the crunchy noodle mixture and serve.

Keep leaves fresh

No room for a salad spinner in your luggage? No problem. Wrap salad leaves in a resealable freezer bag or a damp tea towel before chilling and they will stay fresh for 2 to 3 days.

Couscous salad with grapefruit dressing

200ml (7fl oz) vegetable stock
1⅓ cups couscous
2 pink grapefruit
½ bunch of basil leaves, finely chopped
3 sprigs of mint leaves, finely chopped
2 tsp wholegrain Dijon mustard
1 tbsp honey
2 tbsp white wine vinegar
3 tbsp olive oil
salt and freshly ground black pepper
1 leek, quartered lengthways, then cut into
    5mm (¼in) wide pieces
100g (3½oz) cherry tomatoes, halved

1 Bring the stock to the boil in a pan. Stir in the couscous, remove the pan from the heat, and leave the grains to swell for 5 minutes. Fork everything through to separate the grains and leave to stand for a further 5 minutes.

2 Cut the peel off the grapefruit with a knife, making sure the white pith is also removed. Cut segments of fruit between the membranes, working over a bowl while doing this to catch any juice. Once you have segmented the grapefruit, squeeze out any remaining juice and slice each grapefruit segment into 3 pieces.

3 Add the basil and mint to the grapefruit juice along with the mustard, honey, vinegar, and oil. Stir everything together to make the dressing and season to taste with salt and pepper.

4 Combine the couscous, leek, grapefruit, and cherry tomatoes in a bowl and drizzle with the dressing. Divide the salad between 4 plates and serve.

Keep it simple
There are several types of camping cutlery: you can get folding designs, a complete set that fits into a practical bag, cutlery with karabiner hooks for easy attaching, or – for the minimalists – the "spork". A spork is a single piece of cutlery with a fork on one side and a spoon on the other!

Grilled radicchio salad

For the dressing
4 tbsp olive oil
2 tbsp sherry vinegar
2 tsp medium–hot mustard
1 tbsp honey
salt and freshly ground black pepper

For the salad
6 shallots, stems removed, quartered
2 tbsp olive oil
1 radicchio, halved, stalks removed, then
    sliced into 1cm (½in) thick strips
1 small red lollo rosso lettuce, torn into
    bite-sized pieces

1 Put the dressing ingredients into a small bowl and stir. Season to taste with salt and set aside.

2 Brush the shallots with 1 tablespoon of the olive oil, season with salt and pepper, and cook over a hot barbecue grill for 5 minutes. Move to a cooler part of the grill and continue to grill over a low heat for 12 minutes, until the shallots are soft. Close the lid (if you have one) on the barbecue during this process. Remove the shallots from the barbecue grill and set aside.

3 Brush the radicchio with the remaining olive oil and season with salt and pepper. Place the pieces cut-side down and cook for 2–3 minutes over a low heat with the barbecue lid closed if possible, until the edges begin to go brown and crisp. Remove from the grill and leave to cool slightly.

4 Divide the lollo rosso between 4 plates. Scatter the shallots over the lettuce and divide the radicchio evenly between the plates. Drizzle everything with the dressing and serve.

For 4 people
Preparation time about 40 minutes · infusion time 20 minutes

Country potato salad

1.5kg (3lb 3oz) waxy new potatoes, peeled
  if preferred
4 tbsp rapeseed oil
1 red pepper, deseeded and cut into
  3 x 3cm (1½in) pieces
2 red onions, finely sliced
3 tbsp red wine vinegar
4 tbsp mustard
1 tbsp sugar
salt and freshly ground black pepper
½ bunch of flat-leaf parsley, leaves and stems
  roughly chopped

1 Boil the potatoes in salted water for 25 minutes, drain, and leave to cool slightly before cutting into 8 pieces or slicing into approximately 1cm (½in) thick discs.

2 Heat the oil in a large pan on the gas stove or barbecue. Sauté the pepper and onions, stirring constantly, over a moderate heat for 2 minutes. Add the potatoes to the pan and continue to fry for a further 6 minutes.

3 Combine the vinegar, mustard, and sugar in a large bowl. Add the potatoes and vegetables and mix carefully. Season to taste with salt and pepper and leave to stand for 20 minutes.

4 Add the parsley to the potato salad and fold it in. Adjust the salad seasoning with additional salt and pepper, if required, and serve.

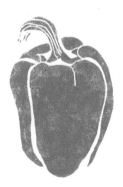

Apple and spinach salad with cranberry dressing

For the dressing

2 tbsp orange marmalade

3 tbsp white wine vinegar

1 tsp medium–hot mustard

salt and freshly ground black pepper

4 tbsp rapeseed oil

3 tbsp dried cranberries

For the salad

5 handfuls of baby spinach, stalks removed
and leaves torn

1 small head of radicchio, stalk removed,
quartered, and sliced diagonally into
5mm (¼in) strips

1 red onion, cut into wafer-thin strips

2 apples, such as Granny Smith, core
removed, cut into 3mm (⅛in) slices

3 tbsp pecans or pumpkin seeds, roughly
chopped

1 Stir together the marmalade, vinegar, mustard, 1 teaspoon of
salt, and 2 pinches of pepper in a salad bowl until the salt has
dissolved. Add the oil and cranberries and stir.

2 Add the spinach, radicchio, sliced onion, and apples to the salad
bowl and combine with the dressing. Season the salad to taste
with additional salt and pepper, if required, and divide between
4 plates. Scatter with the chopped nuts or seeds and serve.

Voyage of discovery

Shopping abroad is much more fun than
at home. You can take your time picking up
your provisions and admire all the regional
specialities and different products. Dive in!
Also, ask at the campsite about weekly
regional markets, where delicious local
produce will await you.

Cooking outdoors - a great experience!

Creating meals in an improvised, open-air kitchen offers an enormous amount of freedom. Even dealing with the stove is part of the whole camping experience – it's a real outdoor adventure!

Camping stoves are ten a penny, so it can be difficult deciding which one is best for your needs. Every camper has their own preconceptions and will gladly talk shop on the subject. The crucial thing when choosing your equipment is to work out what your requirements are.

Safe, clean, and simple gas stoves:

Various types of fuel can be used for heating up your food. A popular camping option is a gas stove. These come in a number of different sizes, with one or two burners, and can be run using butane, propane, or some combination of these fuels. They are super easy to use! You can get pierceable gas canisters, or valve canisters with screw or clip-fit connectors. A gas stove isn't heavy; on average they weigh 77g (2½oz). The canisters are rather heavier and you should ideally have a spare one as a back-up. Energy-saving solutions are particularly popular for campers, because the lower the fuel consumption, the fewer supplies you need to pack. As long as you have an adequate supply of gas, you will be ensured a reliable mode of cooking and high performance that will bring a litre of water to the boil in about 5 minutes.

Reliable petrol stoves

It takes extreme cold to impact on the performance of petrol stoves, which perform very well even in icy temperatures. Another advantage is that petrol can be bought everywhere. However, these camping stoves are not quite as convenient to use as gas stoves; they emit a stronger smell and always have to be cleaned thoroughly. One possible solution for a round-the-world trip or an expedition is the multi-fuel stove, which is designed to run on either petrol or butane or propane.

Other options

Another fairly reliable option is the spirit stove. The downside of these is that they aren't as easy to control, they have only a moderate heat output, and they can cause a build-up of soot on your pans. Solid fuel stoves, which run on hexamine fuel tablets, are small and lightweight. They are suitable for simple meals that just need warming up. Electric stoves always require a power connection at the campsite. They are very simple to operate and function exactly like a normal stove, but are very restricting.

Five practical camping stove tips

1. Read the operating instructions and practise before you set off.
2. Acquire a windbreak.
3. Use the equipment outside (unless specifically suited for indoor use).
4. Make sure the stove is secure when you set it up.
5. Don't forget the saucepan lid – it will save energy.

Decision-making guide when purchasing

Ask yourself the following questions and seek advice accordingly:

Where am I travelling to? Not all countries (especially outside Europe) sell suitable gas canisters.

How am I getting from A to B? Flammable substances such as gas, petrol, meths, or alcohol are prohibited in aircraft.

Where will I be cooking once there? Different conditions will apply on a trek through the Himalayan mountains than at a family-friendly campsite in France.

How much does my luggage weigh? Choose the number and weight of your stoves and cannisters accordingly.

Fettuccine "Alfredo"

1 onion
2 carrots, peeled
1 leek, sliced lengthways
3 celery stalks
200g (7oz) ham
2 tbsp butter
2 cups cream
2 tsp cornflour
500g (1lb 2oz) fettuccine
½ bunch of flat-leaf parsley, stalks removed
   and leaves roughly chopped
100g (3½oz) Parmesan, finely grated
salt and freshly ground black pepper

1 Chop all the vegetables and the ham into 5mm (¼in) cubes.

2 Melt the butter in a pan over a moderate heat. Add the vegetables and diced ham and sauté for 3 minutes, stirring constantly. Add the cream then stir the cornflour into 100ml (3½oz) water and add this, too. Simmer over a low heat, stirring occasionally, for 15 minutes.

3 While the sauce is cooking, bring 2 litres (3½ pints) of salted water to the boil in a second pan. Cook the fettuccine according to the packet instructions until al dente.

4 Add the parsley to the sauce at the end of the cooking time along with the Parmesan. Stir and season to taste with salt and pepper.

5 Drain the fettuccine and divide between 4 plates. Serve the pasta with the sauce.

One-pot cuisine
If you would you like to make the pasta in a single pan just proceed as described above, but before the simmering stage in Step 2, add the pasta to the pan. Pour over enough vegetable stock to cover all the ingredients then cook everything over a moderate heat, stirring occasionally. If too much liquid boils off, just add a bit more water.

Pasta Bolognese alla Nonna

2 tbsp olive oil
250g (9oz) minced beef
1 onion, finely diced
1 garlic clove, finely chopped or crushed
400g (14oz) passata
3 tbsp sugar
2 tsp chilli flakes
salt
400g (14oz) spaghetti
½ bunch of basil, stalks removed and
  leaves chopped
100g (3½oz) hard cheese, such as
  Parmesan, Pecorino, or Gruyère,
  coarsley grated

1 Heat the oil in a pan. Fry the minced meat over a high heat for about 5 minutes until browned. Add the onion and garlic and continue to fry for another 2 minutes.

2 Add the passata to the pan along with the sugar and chilli flakes and stir gently. Cover the pan with a lid and simmer over a low heat for 15 minutes, stirring occasionally.

3 While the sauce is cooking, bring 2 litres (3½ pints) of salted water to the boil in a second pan. Cook the spaghetti according to the packet instructions until al dente.

4 Add the basil to the sauce and season to taste with salt.

5 Drain the spaghetti in a sieve and divide between 4 plates. Serve with the sauce and the cheese scattered on top.

A meandering journey
If you need to get somewhere fast, the motorway is usually the quickest route. But if you want to make the most of your holiday destination, we suggest taking alternative routes now and then. Some country roads have breathtaking views that can make the journey as enjoyable as the destination.

Goulash with paprika and potatoes

2 tbsp rapeseed oil
500g (1lb 2oz) mixed strips of beef and pork
salt and freshly ground black pepper
3 onions, diced
2 garlic cloves, finely chopped or crushed
2 tbsp flour
2 tbsp tomato purée
1 tbsp beef (or other meat) stock, or 1 beef
   stock cube
1 tsp caraway
2 tsp paprika
2 red peppers, deseeded and cut into
   3cm (1½in) cubes
8 waxy potatoes, peeled and quartered
4 tbsp sour cream

1 Heat the oil in a pan. Season the meat with salt and pepper and sauté over a high heat for 8 minutes, until browned. Add the diced onion and continue to fry over a moderate heat for a further 5 minutes. Stir in the garlic and flour and sweat for 1 minute, then stir in the tomato purée and cook for 3 minutes.

2 Pour in 400ml (14fl oz) cold water, add the stock, caraway, and paprika, cover, and leave to stew over a low heat for 40 minutes. Then add the peppers to the pan and stew for another 20 minutes.

3 Add the potatoes to a second pan. Cover with water, season with 1 teaspoon of salt, bring to the boil, and cook for 20 minutes, then drain.

4 Season the goulash to taste with salt and pepper and divide between 4 plates. Garnish each portion with 1 tablespoon of sour cream and serve with the potatoes.

 For 2 people · preparation time about 35 minutes

Pan-fried sausage and leek with potatoes

1 tbsp butter
400g (14oz) waxy potatoes, peeled
  and cut into 5mm (¼in) strips
2–4 smoked sausages (about 150g/
  5½oz), cut into 1cm (½in) slices
1 leek, halved lengthways then sliced
  diagonally into thin strips
2 red onions, sliced into thin strips
1 large beef tomato, cut into 2cm
  (¾in) cubes
4 tbsp soft cheese with herbs
salt and freshly ground black pepper

1 Heat the butter in a large pan. Sauté the potatoes and sausages over a moderate heat for 5 minutes, stirring constantly. Add the leek and onions and continue to fry for a further 3 minutes. Add the diced tomatoes to the pan, stir, and cook everything for an additional 10 minutes over a moderate heat, stirring occasionally.

2 Stir in the soft cheese until it has completely dissolved. Season to taste with salt and pepper, divide between 2 plates, and serve.

Croque Madame

2 tsp Dijon mustard
2 tbsp crème fraîche
8 slices white bread
4 slices of ham
4 slices of Gruyère cheese
4 tbsp butter
4 eggs
salt and freshly ground black pepper

1 Stir the mustard and crème fraîche together. Spread this thinly over the slices of bread. Top 4 of the slices with ham and cheese. Cover with the remaining 4 slices of bread and press down slightly. Heat some of the butter in a pan and fry the croques in batches over a moderate heat for 2–3 minutes each side.

2 Meanwhile heat the remaining butter in a second pan and fry the eggs. Season with salt and pepper. Divide the croques between 4 plates, top with the fried eggs, and serve.

Do eggs really need to go in the fridge?
Obviously space is at a premium in a camping kitchen, but ideally eggs should be stored in a fridge. Their natural protective layer means they will keep unrefrigerated for 18 days after they are laid, but when you're travelling it's best to err on the safe side and get them chilled right away. Once eggs have been refrigerated, they will stay fresh for longer.

Three omelette options

Spanish omelette

6 eggs
salt and freshly ground black pepper
100g (3½oz) chorizo, cut into
    small cubes
1 red pepper, deseeded and cut into
    small cubes
1 waxy potato, cut into small cubes
2 tbsp butter

1 Crack 3 of the eggs into a bowl, season with salt and pepper, and whisk gently with a fork then set aside. In a separate bowl, combine the chorizo, pepper, and potato.

2 Heat 1 tablespoon of the butter in a pan (24cm/9½in diameter) over a moderate heat until it foams. Add half the chorizo mixture and fry for 6 minutes, stirring occasionally. Add the beaten eggs and tilt the pan to distribute evenly. Cover and cook the omelette for about 3 minutes. Carefully fold it over using a spatula and continue to cook, covered, for a further 3 minutes.

3 Slide the omelette onto a plate and wrap the plate in a clean tea towel to keep it warm. Make a second omelette, as above, from the remaining chorizo mixture and eggs.

Austrian omelette

100g (3½oz) streaky bacon, cut
    into strips
6 eggs
salt and freshly ground black pepper
100g (3½oz) hard cheese, such
    as Emmental or Parmesan,
    coarsley grated

1 Add half the bacon to a dry pan (24cm/9½in diameter) and sauté over a moderate heat until crisp all over.

2 Crack 3 of the eggs into a bowl, season with salt and pepper, and whisk gently with a fork. Add the eggs and half the cheese to the pan and tilt to distribute evenly. Cover the pan and cook the omelette for 3 minutes. Carefully fold it over using a spatula and continue to cook, covered, for a further 3 minutes.

3 Slide the omelette onto a plate and and wrap the plate in a clean tea towel to keep it warm. Make a second omelette from the remaining ingredients, as above.

Swedish omelette

200g (7oz) cooked prawns
1 garlic clove, finely chopped
  or crushed
2 tbsp olive oil
6 eggs
salt and freshly ground black pepper
½ bunch of dill, finely chopped

1 Tip the prawns into a sieve, rinse, and leave to drain. Stir the garlic into the olive oil. Crack 3 of the eggs into a bowl, season with salt and pepper, and whisk gently with a fork.

2 Heat 1 tablespoon of the garlic oil in a pan (24cm/9½in diameter) and sauté half the prawns over a moderate heat on all sides. Add the beaten eggs and tilt the pan to distribute evenly. Cover the pan and cook the omelette for 3 minutes. Carefully fold it over using a spatula and continue to cook, covered, for a further 3 minutes.

3 Slide the omelette onto a plate and and wrap the plate in a clean tea towel to keep it warm. Cook the remaining prawns and egg mixture in the leftover butter to make a second omelette, as above. Sprinkle the cooked omelettes with the dill and serve immediately.

Cheese and vegetable gnocchi

2 cups flour
200g (7oz) Gouda cheese, roughly grated
1 tsp ground turmeric
salt and freshly ground black pepper
100g (3½oz) sugar snap peas, halved
   lengthways then cut into 5mm (¼in) wide
   strips
1 carrot, peeled and coarsely grated
2 tbsp vegetable stock

1 Stir the flour into 200ml (7fl oz) water in a bowl. Add the Gouda, turmeric, 1 tsp salt, 2 pinches of pepper, and the vegetables and work with your hands to combine. Leave to stand for 15 minutes.

2 Meanwhile, in a pan bring 1.5 litres (2¾ pints) water to the boil and dissolve the stock in it. Lower the temperature and add 2 teaspoons of the cheesy mixture. Once the entire mixture has been used, leave to steep over a moderate heat for about 12 minutes. Divide the gnocchi between 2 plates and serve with some of the stock.

Frying pan option
You can also use this mixture to make vegetable and cheese flatbreads in a frying pan. To do this, heat some oil, add about 1 tbsp of the mixture to the pan for each flatbread, and fry for 4 minutes on each side over a moderate heat.

For 2 people
Preparation time about 25 minutes

Greek pan-cooked pasta

100g (3½oz) orzo (rice-shaped pasta pieces)
3 tbsp olive oil
1 aubergine, cut into about 2cm (¾in) cubes
1 courgette, cut into about 2cm (¾in) cubes
1 red onion, finely diced
1 garlic clove, finely chopped or crushed
3 tomatoes, quartered
200g (7oz) feta cheese, cut into 2cm (¾in)
  cubes
2 tsp dried oregano
½ tsp dried thyme
salt and freshly ground black pepper

1 Cook the pasta in a pan with 500ml (16fl oz) salted water according to the packet instructions. Pour into a sieve, rinse in cold water, and leave to drain.

2 Heat the oil in a large pan. Sauté the aubergine and courgette in the pan over a high heat for 3 minutes, stirring constantly. Lower the temperature to a moderate heat. Add the onion and garlic to the vegetables and fry for a further 3 minutes. Add the tomatoes, deglaze with 4 tablespoons of water, reduce the temperature to a low heat, and continue cooking for a further 10 minutes.

3 Add the pasta, feta, oregano, and thyme to the vegetables in the pan and heat for 2 minutes. If needed, add 1–2 tablespoons of water to prevent the pasta from sticking. Season to taste with salt and pepper and serve.

Vegetable favourites for when you're on the move
There's always a chronic shortage of space in cool boxes. So when choosing vegetables for a journey, we opt for ones that don't really need to be kept chilled – such as tomatoes, courgettes, or aubergines. This frees up space in our coolbox for items that spoil easily, such as fish, meat, and dairy products.

Vegetable stew with gnocchi

100g (3½oz) bacon, cut into 5mm (¼in)
 wide strips
4 carrots, chopped into 1cm (½in) cubes
2 kohlrabi, chopped into 1cm (½in) cubes
2 onions, finely diced
3 celery stalks, cut into 1cm (½in) pieces
3 tbsp vegetable stock
400g (14oz) potato gnocchi
½ bunch of flat-leaf parsley, leaves roughly
 chopped
salt and freshly ground black pepper

1 Heat a pan without any oil or fat. Fry the bacon over a moderate heat for 3 minutes, stirring constantly. Add the carrots, kohlrabi, onion, and celery and sweat for 3 minutes in the fat that has been released from the bacon.

2 Pour in 1.5 litres (2¾ pints) water, stir in the stock and bring to the boil. Simmer over a low to moderate heat for 20 minutes, stirring occasionally. After 10 minutes add the gnocchi and continue to cook.

3 Add the parsley to the cooked stew, season everything to taste with salt and pepper, divide between 4 plates, and serve.

Into the thermos
Are you off hiking in the mountains, or dashing over hill and dale on your bicycle? Not surprisingly, active campers get absolutely ravenous when they're out trekking or cycling. The perfect solution is a pre-prepared vegetable stew in a vacuum flask. Just decant the cooked dish into a suitable thermos while it is still hot and enjoy it when you take a break – you'll be full of energy when you set off again.

Cauliflower cheese croquettes

For the croquettes
1 cauliflower (about 1kg/2¼lb)
1 onion, finely diced
150g (5½oz) Comté cheese (or Gruyère),
    coarsely grated
½ bunch of flat-leaf parsley, leaves roughly
    chopped
2 eggs
1½ cups white breadcrumbs, plus extra
    if needed
grated nutmeg
salt
1 litre (1¾ pints) rapeseed oil

For the sauce
1 tbsp butter
1 tbsp plain flour
1 tbsp lemon juice
200ml (7fl oz) milk
1 onion, finely diced
bunch of chives, finely chopped
grated nutmeg
salt

1 Split the cauliflower into small florets, wash, and cook in salted water for about 15 minutes, until soft. Drain in a sieve, making sure you retain 200ml (7fl oz) of the cooking water. Leave the cauliflower to cool for 10 minutes.

2 Transfer the cauliflower to a bowl and mash it with a fork or potato masher. Add the onion, cheese, parsley, eggs, and breadcrumbs and work until combined. Season with nutmeg and salt. If necessary add some more breadcrumbs until the mixture is firm enough to shape. Use your hands to make about 20 similar-sized croquettes and set aside.

3 To make the sauce, melt the butter in a pan over a moderate heat, stir in the flour, and cook for 30 seconds. Pour in the lemon juice, milk, and retained cooking water. Add the chopped onion and chives, bring to the boil, stirring constantly, then simmer for 2 minutes over a low heat.

4 Meanwhile, heat the oil in a separate pan. Place the cauliflower croquettes in a deep sieve, lower them into the hot fat, and fry over a moderate heat until golden brown. Remove and leave to drain on kitchen paper.

5 Season the sauce to taste with nutmeg and salt and serve with the croquettes.

Fancy a change?
Instead of making croquettes, you can also shape the mixture into flatbreads and fry them in hot oil in a pan over a moderate heat for 3–4 minutes on each side.

Pasta with cabbage and bacon

400g (14oz) fusilli
100g (3½oz) lard
150g (5½oz) streaky bacon
2 onions, diced
1 head white cabbage (around 500g/
  1lb 2oz), stalk removed and cut into
  2cm (¾in) cubes
1 tsp sugar
½ tsp caraway
1 tsp paprika
salt and freshly ground black pepper

1 Bring 2 litres (3½ pints) salted water to the boil in a pan for the pasta. Cook the pasta in the boiling water according to the packet instructions until al dente.

2 While the pasta water is cooking, melt the lard in a large pan. Fry the bacon and onions over a moderate heat until golden brown. Add the cabbage and cook for about 12 minutes. Sprinkle over the sugar, stir, and allow to caramelize slightly.

3 Season the vegetables with caraway and paprika then add salt and pepper to taste. Tip the pasta into a sieve, leave to drain briefly, then mix with the cabbage in the pan. Divide between 4 plates and serve.

One-pot version
If you have only one burner, the cabbage can be prepared in the same pan used for cooking the pasta. Just add the pasta again at the end, stir everything well, and enjoy.

Born to be wild

Into the wilderness!

If you're looking for somewhere to camp to get back to nature, make sure you find out exactly where you're allowed to pitch a tent. In some countries, such as Spain, wild camping is prohibited, while other countries, such as Sweden, are very relaxed about it. If you are spending the night in a national park, check beforehand whether there is any limit on the number of visitors each day and whether you have to book, where you are allowed to light a fire, and what arrangements there are in terms of water supplies.

What do you need for wild camping?

Whether you are travelling by car or bike or you are on foot, makes a massive difference when you are wild camping. If you are carrying your tent, sleeping bag, and all your cooking equipment in your rucksack, you will obviously be restricted and will need to carry the absolute minimum. Pack only small, lightweight items and make sure that everything is functional and, ideally, waterproof.

Adventurous ingredients

Wild campers have very limited options when it comes to keeping food cool, such as a hole in the ground or a cold stream. In any case, who wants to carry huge quantities of food into the wilderness? Handy, durable snacks are ideal for an occasional energy boost (see recipes from page 24). And once you've worked up a real appetite in the great outdoors you can satisfy your hunger with one of the instant meals on page 90, which need only hot water to rehydrate them. Freeze-dried onions are useful, as are other products such as powdered milk and garlic granules, which can be found in supermarkets. Freeze-dried meat and other more luxurious ingredients can be bought from specialist outdoors shops or online.

Outdoors survival

If you want to immerse yourself truly in nature, you will need to do some thorough research in advance to ensure you are well-informed before you set off on your trip. Carrying water is heavy work, but "wild" water can make you unwell if it isn't collected at the right location or boiled or filtered properly. Also, only eat berries, mushrooms, and herbs that you've collected if you can clearly recognize and identify them and are 100 per cent sure that they are not poisonous.

Wild kitchen

Use the following tips as a guide when cooking over a camp fire:

* use dry wood as fuel.
* before you start cooking, let the fire burn until the combustible material has turned white. Don't cook over flames that are still leaping up!
* use a cast-iron pan that doesn't have any plastic parts. For grilling, place a grill over the embers.
* prepare your ingredients thoroughly in advance, because cooking over a camp fire is a hot business and things cook in a matter of minutes.
* use all the different areas of the fire: different recipes may be best cooked over small flames, or in the embers or the ashes.
* test to see if food is cooked: the cooking time will depend on the heat and the distance from the embers.

"Fast" food from a bag

If you're spending the night in the middle of nowhere, you probably won't want to carry a lot of supplies, so rustling up some freeze-dried food is really convenient. Instant dishes that you just pour water on to rehydrate used to be very popular. However, home-made versions not only taste a whole lot better, they also offer far more variety and are pretty cool. These mini-gourmet meals are definitely soul-food from a bag!

Instant couscous with apricots and macadamia nuts

2 tbsp macadamia nuts, roughly chopped
3 tbsp dried apricots, quartered
5 tbsp couscous
2 tbsp freeze-dried diced chicken
1½ tsp chicken stock, or 1 chicken stock cube
¼ tsp dried thyme
¼ tsp garlic granules
1 tsp onion granules
2 pinches of ground black pepper

1 Toast the nuts in a dry pan until golden brown. Place all the ingredients in a freezer bag and seal.

2 Bring 350ml (12fl oz) water to the boil in a pan then remove from the hob. Add the contents of the freezer bag, stir, and leave to stand for 6–8 minutes, stirring occasionally.

Instant curry rice with cashews

3 tbsp cashews
1 cup par-boiled pre-cooked basmati rice
2 tbsp freeze-dried diced chicken
3 tbsp freeze-dried mixed vegetables
1½ tsp chicken stock, or 1 chicken stock cube
1½ tsp curry powder
1 tsp onion granules
¼ tsp garlic granules
2 pinches of ground black pepper

1 Toast the cashews in a dry pan until golden brown. Add all the ingredients to a freezer bag and seal.

2 Bring 350ml (12fl oz) water to the boil in a pan. Stir in the contents of the freezer bag, remove the pan from the heat, and cover with a lid. Leave to stand for 9 minutes, stirring everything well after 3–4 minutes.

Creamy instant noodles with mushrooms and pine nuts

2 tbsp pine nuts
2 handfuls vermicelli (about 80g/2¾oz)
2 tbsp freeze-dried diced chicken
2 tbsp dried mushrooms
1½ tsp chicken stock, or 1 chicken stock cube
3 tbsp ready-grated Parmesan
2 tbsp powdered milk
2 tsp cornflour
2 tsp herbes de Provence
¼ tsp garlic granules
2 pinches of ground black pepper

1 Toast the pine nuts in a dry pan until golden brown. Add all the ingredients to a freezer bag and seal.

2 Put the contents of the freezer bag into a pan with 300ml (10fl oz) water. Bring to the boil while stirring, then remove from the hob and cover with a lid. Leave to stand for 9 minutes, stirring everything well after 3–4 minutes.

Mexican instant rice with chicken

1 cup par-boiled basmati pre-cooked rice
2 tbsp freeze-dried diced chicken
3 tbsp freeze-dried sweetcorn
2 tbsp freeze-dried tomatoes
1½ tsp chicken stock, or 1 chicken stock cube
1½ tsp chilli flakes
¼ tsp ground cumin
¼ tsp dried oregano
½ tsp ground coriander
1 tsp onion granules
¼ tsp garlic granules
2 pinches of ground black pepper

1 Add all the ingredients to a freezer bag and seal.

2 Bring 350ml (12fl oz) water to the boil in a pan, then remove from the hob. Stir in the contents of the freezer bag and leave to stand for 6–8 minutes, stirring occasionally.

Chicken and vegetable mix with sautéed potatoes

340g can sweetcorn
6 tbsp rapeseed oil
8 waxy potatoes, cut into 5mm (¼in) thick slices
500g (1lb 2oz) chicken breast fillet, cut into 3cm (1½in) cubes
3 carrots, peeled and chopped into 2cm (¾in) cubes
2 red peppers, deseeded and cut diagonally into 1cm (½in) thick strips
2 celery stalks, cut diagonally into 1cm (½in) thick strips
1 onion, diced
1 red chilli, deseeded and finely chopped
2 tbsp honey
2 tbsp soy sauce
salt and freshly ground black pepper

1 Empty the sweetcorn into a sieve, rinse, and leave to drain. Heat 4 tablespoons of the oil in a pan. Sauté the sliced potato over a moderate heat for 25 minutes, turning occasionally but not too often so the potatoes turn nice and crisp.

2 After about 10 minutes, heat the remaining oil in a pan. Fry the chicken breast over a high heat for 1 minute on both sides. Add all the vegetables, except the diced onion, and continue to fry for 3 minutes, stirring constantly. Add the chilli, honey, and soy sauce to the chicken pan, stir, and then pour in 100ml (3½fl oz) water. Cover with a lid and cook over a low heat for 10 minutes. Remove the lid and simmer over a high heat until the liquid has almost entirely evaporated. Season to taste with salt and pepper.

3 About 5 minutes before the end of the potato cooking time, add the chopped onion to the potatoes and continue to cook. Season the potatoes to taste with salt and pepper. Arrange with the chicken and vegetable mix on 4 plates and serve.

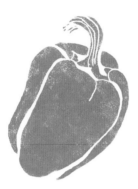

Sweet potato and pepper stew

400g can butter beans
2 tbsp butter
1 garlic clove, finely chopped or crushed
1 large sweet potato (about 350g/12oz),
  peeled and cut into 2cm (¾in) cubes
1 red pepper, deseeded and cut into
  1cm (½in) wide strips
1 yellow pepper, deseeded and cut into
  1cm (½in) wide strips
2 celery stalks, cut into 2cm (¾in)
  wide pieces
2 tomatoes, quartered
3 sprigs of sage leaves, sliced into thin strips,
  or 2 tsp dried sage
salt and freshly ground black pepper

1 Pour the beans into a sieve, rinse, and leave to drain.

2 Heat the butter in a pan. Sweat the garlic over a moderate heat for 1 minute. Add the sweet potato cubes, peppers, and celery and sauté for 3 minutes, stirring constantly. Add the tomatoes and beans then pour in 100ml (3½fl oz) water and stir. Cover the pan with a lid and simmer over a low heat for 12 minutes.

3 Add the sage to the vegetables then season the stew with salt and pepper. Divide between 2 plates and serve.

Rattling in the box
To prevent camping glasses and cups from constantly clattering while you are driving, use plate, cup, and glass holders, available from specialist shops. If you don't have a kitchen cupboard while camping, use a large, sealable, plastic box to store your utensils. These kinds of storage containers can be stacked up brilliantly in your mobile home.

Spicy minced meat risotto

3½ tbsp Parmesan, finely grated
1 tbsp rapeseed oil
250g (9oz) minced meat, your choice of
  beef, pork, veal, or turkey
1 onion, finely diced
2 garlic cloves, finely chopped or pressed
2 red chillies, deseeded and finely chopped
2 cups risotto rice
1 tbsp vegetable stock
salt and freshly ground black pepper
2 tbsp sour cream, to garnish

1 Put the Parmesan in a bowl and set aside. Heat the oil in a pan. Sauté the minced meat over a high heat until it begins to brown. Add the onion, garlic, and chilli and fry for 2 minutes. Stir in the rice followed by 3 cups of warm water.

2 Stir in the stock, reduce the temperature, and simmer over a low heat for 20 minutes, stirring occasionally. If the liquid cooks off before the rice has cooked, add some more water a tablespoon at a time. Ideally all the liquid should have been absorbed by the rice at the end of the cooking time.

3 Take the pan off the heat and fold the Parmesan into the risotto. Season to taste with salt and pepper and divide the risotto between 2 plates. Garnish each portion with 1 tablespoon of sour cream and serve.

Minced meat is the best!
Minced meat is a real diva when compared with other meat. This sensitive soul should be bought fresh on the day you intend to cook it. If you buy shrink-wrapped mince, make sure you observe the best-before date on the pack. And always keep it chilled!

Paella

300g (10oz) mussels
8 chicken drumsticks
salt and freshly ground black pepper
2 tbsp olive oil
1 red onion, cut into fine strips
2 garlic cloves, finely chopped or crushed
1½ cups risotto rice
250ml (9fl oz) dry white wine
1 tbsp chicken stock, or 1 chicken stock cube
about 1g saffron
2 bay leaves
1 red pepper, deseeded and cut into fine
   strips
12 prawns, shelled and head removed
200g (7oz) peas, shelled
1 lemon, cut into quarters, to serve

1 Discard any damaged or open mussels that fail to close after tapping (see p100). Wash the remaining mussels in cold water and debeard them by pinching the stringy thread between your finger and thumb and firmly jerking it away from the mussel shell.

2 Season the chicken with salt and pepper. Heat the oil in a large, high-sided pan and fry the chicken drumsticks over a moderate heat for about 8 minutes, until golden brown on all sides. Transfer to a bowl and set aside.

3 Add the onion and garlic to the same pan and sweat over a moderate heat for 3 minutes, stirring constantly. Add the rice and cook for 2 minutes before deglazing with the wine. Dissolve the stock and saffron in 500ml (16fl oz) hot water and add to the pan. Add the bay leaves and chicken drumsticks, cover with a lid, and cook over a low heat for 10 minutes.

4 Add the mussels and strips of pepper to the pan, stir, and replace the lid. Cook for a further 5 minutes, then stir in the prawns and peas, cover again, and cook for 5 minutes. Season to taste with salt and pepper and serve with the lemon quarters.

Mussels in white wine

2kg (4½lb) mussels
6 tbsp olive oil
2 garlic cloves, lightly crushed
4 onions, sliced into strips
1 leek, sliced lengthways into thin strips
2 carrots, peeled and thinly sliced
4 celery stalks, thinly sliced
1 chilli, deseeded and finely chopped
5 sprigs of thyme
½ tsp salt and 2 pinches of freshly ground
    black pepper
250ml (9fl oz) white wine
bunch of flat-leaf parsley, leaves roughly
    chopped
baguette, to serve (optional)

1 Discard any damaged or open mussels that fail to close after tapping (see below). Wash the remaining mussels in cold water and debeard them by pinching the stringy thread between your finger and thumb and firmly jerking it away from the mussel shell.

2 Heat the olive oil in a large pan with plenty of room for the vegetables and mussels. Sauté the garlic, onions, leek, carrots, celery, chilli, and thyme over a moderate heat for 5 minutes. Season with the salt and pepper. Pour in the white wine and bring to the boil.

3 Add the mussels to the pan and cook, covered, over a moderate heat for 15 minutes.

4 Once the mussels are cooked, add the chopped parsley and stir. Serve the mussels with the vegetable and white wine broth. If available, a fresh baguette goes brilliantly with this.

The tap test
To test whether an open mussel is still alive and fresh, tap it gently on a hard surface. If the mussel closes up in response, it's alive and okay to eat. If it doesn't, then discard it.

Cod in a herby vegetable broth

2 potatoes, peeled and chopped into
   1cm (½in) cubes
1 small fennel bulb, stem removed, cut into
   5mm (¼in) strips
1 carrot, peeled, halved lengthways, then cut
   into 1cm (½in) thick pieces
2 celery stalks, cut into 1cm (½in) thick
   pieces
1 small leek, sliced lengthways then cut into
   2cm (¾in) wide strips
sprig of rosemary
2 sprigs of thyme
3 sprigs of lemon balm
1 garlic clove, lightly crushed
300g (10oz) cod fillet (or another type of
   fish), sliced into 3cm (1½in) wide pieces
salt and freshly ground black pepper
½ bunch of flat-leaf parsley, leaves finely
   chopped, to garnish
2 tbsp olive oil, to garnish

1 Put the vegetables into a pan and cover with 1 litre (1¾ pints) water. Bring to the boil over a high heat, then cover and leave to simmer over a low heat for about 8 minutes. Add the rosemary, thyme, and lemon balm to the pan along with the garlic.

2 Add the fish to the pan and mix gently with the vegetables. Poach, uncovered, in the broth for about 8 minutes, until cooked. Season to taste with salt and pepper. Remove the sprigs of herbs, serve the stew on 2 deep plates, and garnish each portion with the chopped parsley and 1 tablespoon of oil.

Bannock bread Alsace style

4 radishes, thinly sliced
bunch of chives, sliced into small rings
2 cups plain flour, plus extra for dusting
1 tsp baking powder
150g (5½oz) bacon, cut into small cubes
½ tsp salt
4 tbsp sour cream

1 Mix the radishes and chives together in a bowl and set these aside while you make the dough.

2 Combine the flour, baking powder, bacon, and salt in a bowl. Make a well in the centre and pour in 250ml (9fl oz) water. Use your fingers to work the flour gradually in to the water from the edge. As soon as the mixture comes together knead it vigorously by hand until you have a supple dough.

3 Halve the dough and shape it into 2 balls. Press the balls flat on a floured work surface and pull out the edges with your hands until the flatbreads are the same size as the base of your pan. Cook each one in turn in a non-stick pan, without oil, over a moderate heat for about 6 minutes on each side, turning regularly. Spread each of the cooked breads with 2 tablespoons of sour cream and scatter with the chopped chives and radishes.

Who's the boss?
Do you find that sometimes your dough is too firm and other times too sticky, depending on its mood? Don't worry, this has nothing to do with inadequate baking skills. Every variety of flour behaves a bit differently. Just show the dough who is in charge: to get the perfect consistency you may need to add a bit more water or flour than specified in the recipe.

For 2 people
Preparation time about 30 minutes · proving time 1 hour
· baking time about 35 minutes

Bread rolls from a pan

5 tbsp milk
1 tbsp butter
1 tbsp sugar
1 tsp salt
2 tsp dried yeast
1 egg
2 cups plain flour, plus 2 tbsp
for dusting

1 Put the milk, butter, sugar, and salt into a pan and heat until the butter has melted. Transfer to a bowl and leave to cool for 5 minutes, then stir in the yeast until it has dissolved. Leave to stand for about 10 minutes, until the yeast starts to bubble. Add the egg and stir until smooth. Gradually mix in the flour until you have a stiff dough. Dust the dough with the 2 tablespoons of flour and knead it until it is supple. Cover and leave to prove in a warm place for 1 hour.

2 Divide the dough into 4 equal-sized portions and shape these into balls on a lightly floured work surface.

3 Heat a non-stick pan without any oil. Add the dough balls to the pan and cover with a lid. Bake at a moderate heat for 1 minute then reduce the temperature and continue cooking over a low heat for a further 5 minutes.

4 Turn the rolls and continue cooking for another 8 minutes over a low heat, then turn again and bake for a further 8 minutes. Turn the rolls once more, switch off the stove, and leave the rolls resting in the closed pan for 10 minutes.

All together now: cheeeeese!

If you've bought cheese from a deli counter to have with your bread rolls, make sure different cheese varieties are kept separated from each other. Wrap each cheese in foil then make tiny holes in the foil to allow the cheese to breathe – unless the cheese is particularly smelly, in which case the foil is best left intact.

Stuffed flatbreads

2 cups plain flour, plus extra for dusting
¼ tsp baking powder
salt and freshly ground black pepper
50g (1¾oz) salami, cut into small cubes
50g (1¾oz) Gouda cheese, coarsely grated
2 tbsp rapeseed oil

1 Mix the flour and baking powder and a pinch each of salt and pepper in a bowl. Make a well in the centre of the flour and add 140ml (4¾fl oz) water. Gradually stir the flour into the water until the mixture forms a stiff dough, then continue to knead the dough until it is supple.

2 Split the dough into 4 equal-sized portions. Shape these into balls then use a rolling pin to roll them out on a floured work surface into discs measuring about 15cm (6in) in diameter. Alternatively mould them into shape with the ball of your hand.

3 Top half the dough circles with salami and cheese. Fold the other dough halves over the top and press the edges together firmly with the prongs of a fork.

4 Heat the oil in a pan and cook the flatbreads on each side over a moderate heat, with the pan covered, for about 5 minutes, turning two or three times during this process.

Beach paradise

Camping on the beach is so romantic – lying in your tent at night listening to the waves lapping is an unforgettable experience. To make sure it really is paradise, pitch your tent on soft sand. And don't forget to check the high tide mark – you must know how high the water could come in extreme circumstances. In some places you can even rent a beach hammock and sleep under the star-studded sky. What a dream!

Pan-cooked apple cake

2 tart apples, peeled, cored, and thinly sliced
1 cup sugar, plus 2 tbsp
1 tbsp oil
zest and juice of ½ lemon
150g (5½oz) soft butter
3 eggs
2 cups plain flour
2 tsp cocoa powder
2 tsp baking powder
½ tsp ground cinnamon
1 tbsp icing sugar

1 Put the apples in a pan (26cm/10½in diameter) with the 2 tablespoons of sugar and the oil and lemon juice and cook over a moderate heat for 8 minutes, stirring occasionally to prevent the apples from burning.

2 Meanwhile, add the butter, cup of sugar, eggs, and lemon zest to a bowl and stir until well combined. Combine the flour, cocoa, baking powder, and cinnamon and stir this in. Spread the mixture over the apples, smooth the surface, and cover the pan with a lid. Bake over a moderate heat for 5 minutes, then continue cooking over the lowest heat for about another 20 minutes until the cake is cooked.

3 Turn the cake out of the pan using a plate to help, leave to cool slightly, dust with icing sugar, and serve.

For 4 people · preparation time about 25 minutes

French toast with coconut and mango salad

For the mango salad
2 mangoes, stone removed and cut into
   3mm (⅛in) thick slices
1 tbsp lemon juice
2 tbsp honey
4 tbsp coconut milk

For the strips of bread
400g (14oz) one-day-old bread
200g (7oz) or 1 cup condensed milk
1 cup desiccated coconut

1 Put the mango in a bowl with the lemon juice, honey, and coconut
milk. Combine the ingredients well then set aside.

2 To make the toast soldiers, cut the bread into 2cm (¾in) thick slices
and then into 2cm (¾in) wide strips. Put the condensed milk and
desiccated coconut into two deep dishes. Turn the strips of bread first
in the condensed milk, then in the coconut. Toast over a moderate heat
until golden – you can do this on a grill or on a gas stove using a non-stick
pan without oil. Serve the toast with the mango salad.

Fire it up

Feel the warm wind on your skin and the smell of the barbecue in your nostrils as the fire crackles, sizzles, and spits. Yes, it's summer! That open-air feeling plus a barbecue go hand in hand. So don't delay, get grilling!

Barbecue enthusiasts like to get their food fired up over a charcoal grill and swear by the fabulous and unique flavour this imparts. But charcoal barbecues are prohibited for safety reasons on some campsites due to the increased risk of fire caused by flying sparks, so some campers settle for a gas-powered option from the outset. And there's no reason to be disappointed – a gas barbecue has plenty of benefits: it's easy to operate, it heats up in no time, it's no trouble to clean, and the fuel is usually readily available.

Firing up

When barbecuing with charcoal, use special barbecue lighters (eco-friendly options are available) or appropriate natural alternatives. Methylated spirits, petrol, and other chemical substances are a fire hazard so please steer clear of these! If you are using a gas barbecue, to light it up: open the lid and the valve on the gas cylinder, ignite the burners, set them to the highest level, close the lid, and wait for about 10 minutes.

Hot enough?

A charcoal barbecue takes around 30 minutes to heat up. Charcoal is the right choice for brisk, brief barbecuing, but if you want your barbecue to last all evening, use briquettes as they are more durable. So when can you start cooking? If your barbecue doesn't have an integrated thermometer, use this trick to help. Hold the palm of your hand at roughly beer bottle height above the grill. If you need to pull it away after 4 seconds, the barbecue is at a high enough heat (230°C/450°F or above) for steaks. If you can withstand 5–7 seconds, a moderate heat has been reached (175°C/ 347°F or above), the optimum temperature for fish. And if you can last 8–10 seconds, you can barbecue delicate foods such as vegetables at a lower heat (120°C/248°F or above). Ideally, cook with the lid closed so your food is enveloped by heat and aroma from all sides.

Top 5 barbecue accessories

1. Barbecue tongs for turning meat, fish, and vegetables
2. A grill tray or foil for vegetables and other small items
3. Meat thermometer for testing
4. Grill brush to clean the barbecue
5. Silicon brush for oiling and marinating

Grilling options

Do you know the difference between direct and indirect grilling?

Direct grilling: the food is positioned above the embers or the burner. This is ideal for searing steaks or hamburgers, for example.

Indirect grilling: you slide the embers to the side or switch off the burner so the food isn't above direct heat. This is good for slow cooking meat such as spare ribs. We also recommend cooking directly first above the flames, then finishing off with indirect heat until done.

Skewer it up!

We just love barbecuing with skewers! But metal skewers get hot very quickly and have to be handled using gloves, so usually we use the wooden variety in our recipes. Soak the skewers in water for at least 30 minutes before you add the ingredients to avoid them burning on the barbecue. If you have a freezer compartment in your caravan, soaked wooden skewers can be frozen and don't need to be re-immersed in water before use.

BBQ chicken in orange marinade

For the chicken

3 tbsp orange marmalade
4 tbsp BBQ sauce (shop-bought or home-made, see recipe p16)
2 tbsp soy sauce
4 chicken breast fillets (150g/5½ each)

For the vegetables

3 red peppers, deseeded and cut into 3cm (1½in) cubes
2 red onions, cut into thick strips
1 tbsp olive oil
1 tbsp honey
salt and freshly ground black pepper

Also

8 pieces foil (30 × 30cm/12 x 12in each)

1 Stir the marmalade, BBQ sauce, and soy sauce in a bowl and marinate the chicken breast for at least 1 hour, or ideally overnight.

2 Put the peppers and onions into a large bowl with the oil and honey. Season with 1 teaspoon of salt and a pinch pepper and mix well. Lay a piece of foil on top of another then repeat with the rest of the foil pieces to create 4 thick foil sheets. Divide the vegetable mixture evenly between them, spreading it in the centre of each sheet. Fold up the foil and scrunch the open sides together to seal the parcels.

3 Remove the chicken breast from the marinade, season with some salt and pepper, and grill on each side over a moderate heat for 5 minutes. At the same time, lay the pepper packages on the grill and cook over a moderate heat for 10 minutes, turning occasionally to ensure the vegetables cook evenly. Remove from the grill and leave to rest for 5 minutes. Divide between 4 plates and serve along with the chicken breast.

4 This dish can also be cooked in a pan on a gas stove. To do this, heat 1 tablespoon of rapeseed oil in a pan. Fry the chicken breast over a moderate heat for 5 minutes on each side. Meanwhile, heat 1 tablespoon of rapeseed oil in a separate pan and cook the vegetables over a moderate heat for about 10 minutes, stirring occasionally.

One-pan power

You may be wondering how many pans you need while camping. One pan at least is definitely helpful, allowing you to make a range of dishes so you're not always cooking the same thing. Otherwise, the number of pans you take will depend on how many people you are cooking for and how you are travelling. A backpacker might take a single pan while a family in a camper van has room for at least two different-sized pans.

Stuffed steaks on a ratatouille and carrot base

For the steaks

4 steaks (150g/5½oz each), your choice
   of beef, pork, veal, or turkey
4 tsp medium–hot mustard
4 slices Parma ham
2 sprigs of sage leaves
salt and freshly ground black pepper

For the vegetables

3 tbsp olive oil
2 carrots, peeled, quartered, then sliced
   diagonally into 5mm (¼in) pieces
4 potatoes, peeled, quartered, then sliced
   diagonally into 5mm (¼in) pieces
1 small aubergine, chopped into 2cm (¾in)
   cubes
1 courgette, chopped into 2cm (¾in) cubes
1 red pepper, deseeded and chopped into
   2cm (¾in) cubes
2 tomatoes, chopped into 2cm (¾in) cubes
200g tin chopped tomatoes
1 tbsp sugar
1 tbsp herbes de Provence

1 Use a knife to cut a pocket in each steak and smear the inside of each with 1 teaspoon of mustard. Spread out the Parma ham, lay the sage leaves evenly on top, and roll the slices up. Stuff 1 little Parma ham roll into the pocket in each steak.

2 For the vegetables, put a pan (without any plastic handles) on the grill. Heat the oil in the pan and sauté the vegetables over a moderate heat for 5 minutes. Stir in the tinned tomatoes, sugar, and herbs. Cover and simmer for 12 minutes, stirring occasionally.

4 Season the steaks with salt and pepper and grill them on the barbecue or fry them in a pan over a high heat for about 4 minutes each side. Season the vegetables to taste with salt and pepper and divide between 4 plates. Top the vegetables with the cooked steaks and serve.

Barbecued herby Camembert

1 garlic clove, finely chopped or crushed
1 tbsp olive oil
8 bay leaves
8 sprigs of rosemary
8 sprigs of thyme
8 sprigs of oregano
4 Camembert cheeses
bread or baguette, to serve

Also
4 pieces of kitchen twine, 60cm (24in) each

1 Stir the garlic into the olive oil. Arrange 1 bay leaf and 1 sprig each of rosemary, thyme, and oregano underneath and on top of each Camembert. Tie each one up into a little parcel using kitchen twine.

2 Drizzle the herby Camemberts with the garlic oil and barbecue over a moderate heat for about 4 minutes on each side. Take care to avoid the cheese burning or melting onto the barbecue. The herbs can burn as they won't be eaten.

3 The cheese is ready when it has begun to brown slightly and small blisters are forming on the surface. Arrange the Camembert cheeses on 4 plates, snip off the kitchen twine and remove the herbs. Serve with fresh bread or a baguette.

Red onion confit from the store cupboard
These cheeses go wonderfully with a red onion confit, which you can make at home and take with you in a jar, as you would with jam. To make the confit, peel 8 red onions, slice in half and then into thin strips. Caramelize 1 tbsp sugar in a pan, remove briefly from the hob, add 2 tbsp butter, let it foam and immediately add the onions and stir. Sweat for about a minute, then deglaze with 100ml (3½fl oz) grape juice and 2 tbsp balsamic vinegar. Add 2 cloves, 1 bay leaf, and 2 juniper berries, cover, and braise over a low heat for about 20 minutes, stirring occasionally. Then remove the lid and simmer over a moderate heat until the liquid has boiled down to create a syrupy consistency. Season to taste with salt and freshly ground black pepper and decant into screw-top jars while still hot. Sealed, this will keep unrefrigerated for up to 2 weeks.

Three tenderizing steak marinades

For the yogurt and curry marinade

100g (3½oz) full-fat yogurt
1 garlic clove, finely chopped or crushed
1 tbsp lemon juice
1 tsp medium–hot mustard
1 tbsp curry powder
1 tsp salt
4 tbsp rapeseed oil

For the paprika and mustard marinade

1 small onion, finely diced
2 tbsp wholegrain Dijon mustard
100ml (3½fl oz) apple juice
1 tbsp lemon juice
1 tbsp paprika
1 tsp dried thyme
1 tsp salt
4 tbsp rapeseed oil

For the honey and chilli marinade

2 red chillies, deseeded and finely chopped
1 garlic clove, finely chopped or crushed
2 tbsp white balsamic vinegar
2 tbsp honey
1 tsp medium–hot mustard
1 tsp dried rosemary
1 tsp salt
8 tbsp rapeseed oil

1 To make the yogurt and curry marinade, stir the yogurt, garlic, lemon juice, mustard, curry powder, and salt together in a bowl until the salt has dissolved. Pour in the oil, stir, then add the meat.

2 For the paprika and mustard marinade, place the onion in a bowl. Add all the remaining ingredients, apart from the oil, and stir until the salt has dissolved. Pour in the oil, stir, then add the meat.

3 For the honey and chilli marinade, place the chillies and garlic in a bowl then add the vinegar, honey, mustard, rosemary, and salt and stir everything until the salt has dissolved. Pour in the oil, stir, then add the meat.

Marinating made easy
Ideally meat should be marinated for 2 hours or overnight in freezer bags in the fridge to allow the flavours to blend perfectly. Cuts of meat such as entrecôte, porterhouse, T-bone, fillet steak, or sirloin are naturally very tender, moist, and full of flavour so they also taste fantastic simply seasoned with salt and pepper.

For 4 people · preparation time about 45 minutes · marinating time 2 hours

Grilled corn on the cob

4 fresh sweetcorns
juice of 1 lime
6 tbsp maple syrup
2 tbsp soy sauce
1 tbsp chilli powder

Also
8 toothpicks

1 Par-boil the sweetcorns in plenty of salted water for 10 minutes. Meanwhile, mix the lime juice with the maple syrup, soy sauce, and chilli powder. Place the sweetcorn in the marinade and leave to infuse for 2 hours, turning occasionally.

2 Grill the sweetcorn on the barbecue over a moderate heat until golden brown all over. Then brush liberally with the marinade. To serve, insert a toothpick at each end of the cooked sweetcorns.

 Delicious festival food
No-one wants to leave a festival to go to the supermarket. Before you get there, think about what you would like to eat and pack all the essentials. You can keep it quite simple: just toss a steak or a couple of sausages on the barbecue to go with the grilled corn on the cob and the party-goers will be full and happy before you know it.

For 4 people · preparation time about 20 minutes · soaking time about 30 minutes

Grilled cherry tomato kebabs

3 sausages (about 400g/14oz)
1 onion, finely diced
1 tsp mustard
1 egg
3 tbsp white breadcrumbs
32 cherry tomatoes (or 16 cherry
   tomatoes and 8 small peppers,
   deseeded and halved)
1 tbsp rapeseed oil
salt and freshly ground black pepper

Also
8 wooden skewers, 20cm/8in long

1 Soak the wooden skewers for at least 30 minutes in water. Slice the
sausages in half lengthways, press out the sausage meat, and put it in
a bowl. Add the onion and mix it in along with the mustard, egg, and white
breadcrumbs. Work everything together to create a consistent mixture and
shape into 32 similar-sized balls.

2 On each wooden skewer, alternate 4 cherry tomatoes or 4 pepper
halves and 4 meatballs. Before cooking, brush with a little oil and
season with salt and pepper.

3 Cook on the barbecue or fry in a pan over a moderate heat for about
8 minutes, turning occasionally to cook both sides.

Hot dogs wrapped in bacon

For the sauerkraut salad

200g (7oz) sauerkraut
1 small baby pineapple, cored, flesh removed
    roughly grated
3½ tbsp pineapple juice
2 tsp honey
1 tbsp rapeseed oil
2 tbsp full-fat yogurt
salt and freshly ground black pepper

For the hot dogs

2 slices Emmental
8 hot-dog sausages
16 slices of bacon
8 hot-dog rolls
8 tbsp remoulade sauce

1 Pour the sauerkraut into a sieve, rinse, and leave to drain. Transfer to a bowl and toss through with a fork.

2 Add the pineapple to the sauerkraut. Add the pineapple juice, honey, oil and yogurt and mix well. Season to taste with salt and pepper and set aside.

3 To make the hot dogs, slice the cheese into 5mm (¼in) wide strips. Make a lengthways incision in the sausages, but don't cut them all the way through. Insert the cheese into this incision and wrap each sausage in 2 rashers of bacon. Grill on the barbecue over a moderate heat until the bacon is crispy. Toast the hot-dog rolls for about 10 seconds on each side, then slice them open but don't cut all the way through.

4 Fill each roll with some of the sauerkraut salad and top with a sausage. Garnish each hot dog with 1 tablespoon of the remoulade sauce and serve.

For 4 people
Preparation time about 40 minutes

BBQ goulash

400g (14oz) sirloin, cut into 1cm (½in)
   wide strips
200ml (7fl oz) BBQ sauce (shop-bought or
   home-made, see recipe p16)
400g (14oz) potatoes, peeled and cut into
   large chunks
2 onions, halved, stems removed, then sliced
   lengthways into strips
1 green pepper, deseeded and diced
1 red chilli, deseeded and diced
300g (10oz) green beans, cut into 3cm
   (1½in) long strips

Also
8 pieces foil (30 × 30cm/12 x 12in each)

1 Mix together the sirloin strips and the BBQ sauce in a large bowl. Put the vegetables in the bowl and mix with the sirloin and sauce.

2 Lay a piece of foil on top of another and repeat with the rest of the foil pieces to create 4 thick foil sheets. Divide the meat mixture evenly between them, spreading it in the centre of each sheet. Fold the foil over the mixture, then scrunch the edges together – not too tightly, you need to leave a bit of room.

3 Put the parcels on the grill and cook over a moderate heat, turning occasionally, for about 25 minutes. Serve straight from the parcels or dish up on 4 plates.

Prepping ahead for the barbecue
This dish is great when prepared in advance and tastes even better the longer the flavours have to develop. You can also cook it in a large pan on a gas stove. Heat 2 tbsp rapeseed oil and sauté all the ingredients over a moderate heat for about 20 minutes. Stir as frequently as possible to avoid it catching.

Potato gratin cooked on a camping BBQ

8 waxy potatoes, peel on, cut into 5mm (¼in) thick slices
1 large onion, halved then cut into thin strips
1 garlic clove, finely chopped or crushed
150g (5½oz) Gouda cheese (or Cheddar or Raclette), roughly grated
2–3 pinches of grated nutmeg
salt and freshly ground black pepper
4 tbsp butter

Also
8 pieces foil (30 × 30cm/12 x 12in each)

1 Wash the potatoes very thoroughly before slicing them. Put the potatoes, onion, garlic, and cheese into a large bowl. Season with the nutmeg, 1 teaspoon of salt and a pinch of pepper and mix everything well.

2 Lay a piece of foil on top of another then repeat with the rest of the pieces to create 4 thick foil sheets. Divide the potato mixture evenly between them, spreading it in the centre of each sheet. Top each potato parcel with 1 tbsp butter and fold up the foil, scrunching together the open sides to seal the parcels.

3 Place the parcels on the grill and cook over a moderate heat for 35 minutes, turning the parcels every 10 minutes during the cooking time to ensure the potatoes cook evenly. Remove from the barbecue, leave to rest for 5 minutes, and serve straight out of the foil parcels.

When potatoes travel...
Potatoes don't like the light, so they should be stored in a cool, dark place – a dark cupboard is usually the perfect location. When you're travelling, for example in a camper van, and need to find an alternative storage solution for your potatoes, just wrap them, unwashed, in newspaper!

Makes 4
Preparation time about 1 hour 30 minutes
· proving time 1 hour 30 minutes

Mini pan-cooked flatbreads

7g sachet dried yeast
1 tbsp honey
2 tsp salt
4½ cups plain flour, plus extra
   for dusting
2 tbsp olive oil
2 tsp nigella seeds

1 Stir together the yeast, honey, and 3½ tablespoons of warm water in a bowl until the yeast has dissolved. Leave to stand for about 10 minutes until the yeast starts to bubble. Combine the salt and flour in a large bowl. Add the yeast mixture, olive oil, and 300ml (10fl oz) warm water.

2 Knead everything together by hand, then continue to work the dough for 5 minutes on a floured work surface. The dough should come together to form a ball and no longer stick to your hands. If necessary, add a little more flour to achieve the desired consistency. Return the dough to the bowl, cover, and leave to prove in a warm place for about 1 hour.

3 Remove the dough from the bowl, knead it briefly again on the lightly floured work surface and divide into 4 equal-sized pieces. Shape the pieces of dough into balls, then press them with the ball of your hand to create roughly 1cm (½in) thick flatbreads. Scatter the nigella seeds on top, cover, and leave to prove for a further 30 minutes.

4 Cook the flatbreads in batches on the barbecue over a moderate to high heat for 6–7 minutes on each side. Close the barbecue during cooking (or you can place a saucepan lid over the flatbreads). Remove from the barbecue and wrap in a tea towel to keep the bread warm until all the flatbreads have been cooked. Serve warm as a side dish.

In a pan
These flatbreads can also be cooked in a pan on a gas stove (see photo). Heat a non-stick pan without any oil or fat and cook the flatbreads, covered, in the pan over a medium to low heat for 6–7 minutes on each side.

Pan-fried pork and beef with Mediterranean vegetables

250g (9oz) pork fillets
250g (9oz) rump steak
1 tbsp tomato purée
1 tbsp soy sauce
1 courgette, cut into 1cm (½in) chunks
8 cherry tomatoes, halved
1 small aubergine, sliced lengthways then
  cut into 1cm (½in) thick strips
1 small fennel bulb, stem removed and cut
  into 5mm (¼in) wide strips
1 red onion, cut into 8 wedges
4 tbsp olive oil
2 tsp herbes de Provence
salt and freshly ground black pepper
4 tbsp sour cream, to serve

Also

8 pieces foil (30 × 30cm/12 x 12 each)

1 Before cutting up the meat, remove any excess fat or tendons. Marinate the meat in a bowl with the tomato purée and soy sauce for about 30 minutes.

2 Meanwhile, put the vegetables in a bowl and mix with the oil, herbs, 1 teaspoon of salt, and a pinch of pepper. Add the meat with the marinade and mix everything together thoroughly.

3 Lay a piece of foil on top of another then repeat with the rest of the foil pieces to create 4 thick foil sheets. Divide the meat and vegetable mixture evenly between them, spreading it out in the centre of each sheet. Fold up the foil and scrunch the open sides together to seal your vegetable parcels.

4 Put these onto the grill and cook over a moderate heat for about 25 minutes. Turn the parcels occasionally to ensure everything cooks evenly. Remove from the grill and leave to rest for 5 minutes. Open the foil and serve stright from the foil, topping each parcel with 1 tablespoon sour cream.

On the stove!

This dish can also be prepared in a pan (see photo). Heat 2 tbsp rapeseed oil and fry the strips of meat and vegetables over a moderate heat for about 20 minutes, stirring occasionally. Pan at the ready, steady, go!

Crazy about campfires?

Holding a stick with a piece of dough on the end over the campfire and watching it slowly colour is something that always reminds us of our childhood camping trips and that feeling of impatience that the bread would just never be ready. Those experiences, which fascinated us then, are still a real pleasure today. When people gather around a campfire, their mood lifts immediately. It brings out the romantic in everyone – so let those sparks fly. Our recipes for campfire bread on a stick are irresistible!

Top 10 hottest campfire to-do list

You must try these 10 campfire suggestions at least once in your life:

1. Tell a creepy story.
2. Munch on toasted marshmallows.
3. Explain a natural phenomenon to the kids.
4. Sing a classic campfire song, such as "Wonderwall" by Oasis or "All Summer Long" by Kid Rock.
5. Play one of the above songs on a guitar – or worship someone else who can.
6. Eat a potato that has been cooked in the embers.
7. Collect wood for yourself (at least one piece) and add it to the fire.
8. Sit as quietly as a mouse and listen to the fire crackling and sizzling.
9. Entrust a friend with a genuine secret.
10. Dance like nobody's watching!

Stick-bread options

For the basic dough

7g sachet dried yeast
1 tbsp sugar
1 tsp salt
2 tbsp olive oil
3 cups flour, plus extra for dusting

For the herby stick bread

2 garlic cloves, finely chopped or crushed
4 sprigs of flat-leaf parsley, leaves and
  stalks finely chopped
bunch of chives, chopped into small rings

For the onion stick bread

1 cup fried onions
1 tsp paprika

For the bacon stick bread

1 cup diced ham
1 cup grated Gouda cheese

Also

4 straight wooden sticks from a hazelnut,
beech, or willow tree (each measuring
  about 50cm/20in)

1 To make the dough, stir the yeast, sugar, and salt into 200ml (7fl oz) warm water in a bowl until the yeast has dissolved. Leave to stand for about 10 minutes until the yeast starts to bubble. Stir in the olive oil and gradually add enough flour to create a stiff dough. Add the remaining flour then knead by hand until the dough is supple. Choose one of the five bread versions below, or go directly to step 5.

2 For the herby stick bread, add the garlic and herbs to the dough and knead until well combined.

3 For the onion stick bread, knead the fried onions and paprika into the dough.

4 For the bacon stick bread, knead the ham and cheese into the dough.

5 Leave the dough to prove for 1 hour. Wash the wooden sticks thoroughly with water and, if necessary, scrub them with a brush along the section where the bread dough will be wrapped.

6 Divide the dough into 4 equal-sized portions. Roll out each one by hand on a floured work surface to create a sausage shape about 50cm (20in) long. Wrap the lengths of dough around the prepared end of the sticks and either cook them over the embers of an open campfire, or over the glowing barbecue coals. Turn the wooden sticks frequently while cooking. Depending on the heat and distance from the embers it will take 30–40 minutes for the bread to cook. The bread is ready when it is brown and crisp on the outside and gives a hollow sound when tapped.

BBQ pizza

For the dough

7g sachet dried yeast
1 tsp sugar
½ tsp salt
1 tbsp olive oil
3 cups plain flour, plus extra
   for dusting

For the sauce

2 tbsp dried oregano
pinch of grated nutmeg
2 tbsp sugar
1½ cups passata
salt

For the topping

2 balls of mozzarella
250g (9oz) Gouda cheese
8 slices of ham

1 To make the dough, stir the yeast, sugar, and salt into 175ml (6fl oz) warm water in a bowl until the yeast has dissolved. Leave to stand for about 10 minutes until the yeast starts to bubble. Stir in the olive oil and gradually add enough flour to create a stiff dough. Add the remaining flour then knead by hand until the dough is supple. Cover and leave to prove in a warm place for 1 hour.

2 Meanwhile, for the sauce, stir the oregano, nutmeg, and the sugar into the passata and season to taste with salt. For the topping, drain the mozzarella and cut each ball into 8 slices. Roughly grate the Gouda and tear the ham into bitesize pieces.

3 Divide the dough into 4 equal-sized portions and shape into balls. Roll these out on a floured work surface to about 20cm (8in) diameter using a rolling pin, or press into shape using your hands. Place the flatbreads in batches on the grill, immediately close the lid (or place a pan lid over the pizzas), and cook over a moderate heat for about 1 minute each side. Remove and spread evenly with the sauce, sprinkle over the Gouda, and top each with 4 slices of mozzarella. Divide the ham between the bases and cook the pizzas on the barbecue for a further 3–5 minutes with the lid closed.

4 Since the temperature of every barbecue is different, it's important to check the cooking progress every so often. Lift each pizza and check the colour and consistency of the base. If the dough is getting too dark underneath or is in danger of burning, remove the pizza from the grill, reduce the temperature, and then continue cooking. The pizzas are ready when the base is crisp and the cheese has melted.

Antipasti veggie kebabs BBQ style

For the marinade

1 garlic clove, finely chopped or crushed
small handful of mint, leaves finely chopped
4 tbsp olive oil
zest and juice of ½ lemon
1 tsp dried oregano

For the veggie kebabs

400g can artichoke hearts
1 courgette, sliced lengthways, then cut
   crossways into 16 equal-sized pieces
8 shiitake mushrooms, halved
8 small peppers, deseeded and halved
250g (9oz) halloumi, sliced lengthways then
   cut into 8 equal-sized cubes
salt and freshly ground black pepper

Also

8 wooden skewers (20cm/8in each)

1   Soak the wooden skewers for at least 30 minutes in water. To make the marinade, stir together the garlic, mint, oil, lemon zest, 2 tablespoons of lemon juice, and oregano in a bowl and set aside.

2   Drain the artichoke hearts in a sieve, then slice in half. Slide the vegetable and halloumi chunks onto the wooden skewers so they are evenly distributed and season with salt and pepper. Barbecue over a moderate heat for 3–4 minutes on each side. Brush with the marinade and serve.

3   You can also make the kebabs on a gas stove. To do this, heat 1 tablespoon of the olive oil in a non-stick pan and fry the veggie kebabs over a moderate heat for 3–4 minutes on each side. Brush with the marinade and serve.

Spear with your fork

To juice a lemon without a squeezer requires some manual work! Slice the lemon in half and stick a fork into the flesh a few times – this will make it easy now to squeeze the lemon by hand. Or to make it even easier, stick the fork in the centre of the lemon, then move it up and down and hey presto... the juice just flows out of its own accord.

Cauliflower and courgette kebabs with almond salsa

For the almond salsa

1 shallot, finely diced
1 garlic clove, finely chopped or crushed
3 tbsp capers, finely chopped
100ml (3½fl oz) olive oil
¼ cup ground almonds
2 tbsp chopped flat-leaf parsley
1 tbsp chopped mint
1 tsp dried oregano
1 tsp grated lemon zest
3 tsp lemon juice
salt and freshly ground black pepper

For the kebabs

2 courgettes, ends removed
1 cauliflower, cut into small florets
2 tbsp olive oil
salt

Also

8 wooden skewers (20cm/8in each)

1 Soak the wooden skewers for at least 30 minutes in water. To make the salsa, stir all the ingredients together in a bowl and season to taste with salt and pepper. Set aside.

2 Use a potato peeler to slice the courgette into thin strips. Take 2 strips of courgette, place one on top of the other, and roll them up. Slide the cauliflower florets and courgette rolls on to the wooden skewers, alternating between the two. Brush evenly with the oil and season with salt.

3 Grill over a moderate heat for 10–12 minutes, turning frequently so the kebabs do not burn. Drizzle evenly with the salsa and serve.

4 You can also make the kebabs on a gas stove. To do this, heat 1 tablespoon of olive oil in a non-stick pan and fry the cauliflower kebabs over a moderate heat for 10–12 minutes on all sides.

Grilled garden vegetables

2 tbsp soft butter
1 garlic clove, crushed
3 waxy potatoes, chopped into 1cm (½in)
    pieces
3 carrots, peeled and cut into 5mm (¼in)
    discs
1 kohlrabi, cut crossways into 5mm (¼in)
    slices
150g (5½oz) green beans
¼ tsp dried oregano
¼ tsp ground turmeric
salt and freshly ground black pepper

Also
8 pieces foil (30 ×30cm/12 x 12in each)

1 Melt the butter in a pan on the hot grill. Add the garlic and let it infuse in the butter for 1 minute. Put the vegetables, oregano, and turmeric in a large bowl along with the butter. Season with ½ teaspoon of salt and a pinch of pepper and mix well.

2 Lay a piece of foil on top of another then repeat with the rest of the foil pieces to create 4 thick foil sheets. Divide the vegetable mixture evenly between them, spreading it out in the centre of each sheet. Fold up the foil and scrunch the open sides together to seal the parcels. Put them on the grill and cook over a moderate heat for about 20 minutes. Turn the parcels occasionally to ensure the vegetables cook evenly. Remove from the grill, leave to rest for 5 minutes, then serve in the foil.

Barbecued balsamic bean parcels

2 garlic cloves, crushed
2 tbsp olive oil
2 tsp Dijon mustard
2 tsp maple syrup
2 tbsp balsamic vinegar
salt
600g (1lb 5oz) green or yellow beans, halved
1 red pepper, deseeded, cut into 5mm (¼in)
 strips
1 yellow pepper deseeded, cut into 5mm
 (¼in) strips
¼ cup pine nuts

Also
8 pieces foil (30 × 30cm/12 x 12in each)

1 Put the garlic, oil, mustard, maple syrup, and vinegar into a large bowl and season with ½ teaspoon of salt. Stir in the beans and peppers until they are completely coated in the marinade.

2 Lay a piece of foil on top of another one then repeat with the rest of the foil pieces to create 4 thick foil sheets. Divide the beans evenly between them, spreading them out in the centre of each sheet. Drizzle over the remaining marinade from the bowl. Scatter with the pine nuts, fold up the foil, and scrunch the open sides together to seal the parcels.

3 Place on the barbecue and grill over a moderate heat for 10–12 minutes, turning frequently to prevent the beans from burning. Remove from the grill and leave to rest for 5 minutes then serve in the foil.

For 4 people · preparation time about 15 minutes
Soaking time about 30 minutes · marinating time about 2 hours

Prawn and lime kebabs

600g (1lb 5oz) raw king prawns (about 16–20
  prawns), peeled and head removed
2 garlic cloves, finely chopped or crushed
1 jalapeño chilli, deseeded and finely
  chopped
3 sprigs of coriander, leaves and stalks finely
  chopped
4 tbsp olive oil
1 tbsp raw cane sugar
½ tsp smoked paprika
½ tsp ground cumin
salt and freshly ground black pepper
2 limes

Also
4 wooden skewers (20cm/8in each)

1 Soak the wooden skewers for at least 30 minutes in water. Put the prawns in a bowl and add all the ingredients except the lime. Cover and marinate in a cool place for at least 2 hours.

2 Trim the ends off 1 lime and slice into 5mm (¼in) thick rounds. Cut the second lime lengthways into quarters and set aside. Slide the prawns and lime slices onto the skewers, alternating with 1 prawn and 1 lime. You should end up with 4–5 prawns on each skewer.

3 Barbecue the prawn kebabs over a moderate heat on each side for 3–4 minutes and serve with a lime segment.

4 You can also make the kebabs on a gas stove. To do this, heat 1 tablespoon of olive oil in a non-stick pan and fry the lime kebabs over a moderate heat for 3–4 minutes on each side. Serve each one with a quarter lime segment.

Store-cupboard marinade
You can prepare the marinade while you are still at home. Crush all the ingredients except the oil using a pestle and mortar until you have a fine paste. Add the oil, mix everything well, transfer to a small, sterilized bottle, and seal. Alternatively put all the marinade ingredients into a blender beaker and purée with a hand-held blender until smooth then decant into your container. The marinade will keep unrefrigerated for up to 1 week.

For 4 people
Preparation time about 40 minutes

Salmon in foil with spiced cauliflower

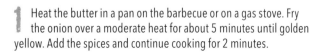

2 tbsp butter
1 onion, finely diced
1 tsp ground ginger
1 tsp garlic granules
1 tsp chilli flakes
2 tsp paprika
2 tsp ground coriander
½ tsp ground cumin
400g can chopped tomatoes
1 small cauliflower, cut into florets
salt and freshly ground black pepper
4 salmon fillets (150g/5½oz each)

Also
8 pieces foil (30 × 30cm/12 x 12in each)

1 Heat the butter in a pan on the barbecue or on a gas stove. Fry the onion over a moderate heat for about 5 minutes until golden yellow. Add the spices and continue cooking for 2 minutes.

2 Add the chopped tomatoes and cauliflower florets and simmer for 8 minutes, stirring occasionally. Season to taste with salt. Remove the pan from the heat, set aside, and leave to cool for 10 minutes. Season the salmon with salt and pepper.

3 Lay one piece of foil on top of another and repeat with the rest of the foil pieces to create 4 thick foil sheets. Divide half of the cauliflower mixture evenly between them, spreading it in the centre of each sheet. Place the fish fillets on top and cover with the remaining cauliflower. Fold up the foil and scrunch the open sides together to seal your parcels.

4 Put these onto the grill and cook over a moderate heat for about 20 minutes, turning every 5 minutes. Remove the parcels from the grill and transfer to 4 plates, opening them up only once you are ready to serve.

Barbecued sea bass

5cm (¼in) piece ginger, peeled
2 garlic cloves
2 sticks of lemon grass, sliced into 2cm (¾in) chunks
1 red chilli, deseeded
4 sprigs of mint, leaves and stalks chopped
piece of star anise
salt and freshly ground black pepper
4 gutted sea bass (300g/10oz each)
4 limes, or lemons, cut into 8 slices

Also

2 old newspapers
4 pieces of kitchen twine (40cm/15½in each)

1 Roughly crush the ginger, garlic, lemon grass, chilli, mint, and star anise in a pestle and mortar or chop with a knife. Season the fish with salt and pepper, including inside the cavity. Distribute the spice mix evenly between the fish, inserting it into the cavity in each one.

2 Lay out the newspaper in 5 equal layers and moisten with a bit of water. Place 4 slices of lime in a row in the centre of each paper stack and place the fish on top, then add the remaining lime slices. Roll up the newspaper firmly and tie each parcel with kitchen twine. Cover the fish parcels completely with salted water and leave to soak for 15 minutes.

3 Grill the fish on the barbecue over a moderate heat for about 15 minutes on each side. To serve, unwrap the fish from the newspaper, remove the herbs and spices from the cavity, and arrange on 4 plates.

Fish ahoy!
There are several ways to cook a whole fish over the campfire and this is a fantastic way to cook fish, be brave! You can wrap the fish in foil and place it in the hot embers. Fish with firm flesh can be put on a skewer held over the coals. Or use a piece of professional grilling kit: a BBQ fish grill holds the fish and makes turning it really easy (see photo).

Lemony salmon with sesame seeds

2 lemons
1 garlic clove, finely chopped or pressed
2 tbsp olive oil
3 tbsp chopped dill
1 tbsp chopped flat-leaf parsley
2 tsp Dijon mustard
1 tsp Worcestershire sauce
600g (1lb 5oz) salmon fillet, cut into 3cm
  (1½in) chunks
2 tbsp sesame seeds
¼ tsp chilli flakes

Also

8 wooden, or metal, skewers (20cm/8in each)

1 If using wooden skewers, soak these for at least 30 minutes in water. Chop a generous chunk off the ends of the lemons and squeeze them by hand then slice the lemons into 5mm (¼in) thick slices. Combine the garlic, lemon juice, oil, dill, parsley, mustard, and Worcestershire sauce in a bowl and set aside.

2 To make the kebabs, hold 2 skewers about 1cm (½in) apart. Slide alternating pieces of salmon and folded slices of lemon on to the skewers. Continue in the same manner with the remaining 6 skewers.

3 Brush the salmon kebabs evenly with the herb and mustard mixture. Mix the sesame seeds and chilli flakes together and scatter all over the salmon kebabs. Grill on the barbecue over a moderate heat for 2 minutes each side then serve.

4 You can also cook the kebabs on a gas stove. To do this, heat 1 tablespoon of olive oil in a non-stick pan and fry the salmon kebabs over a moderate heat for 2 minutes on each side. Serve each kebab with a quarter lemon segment.

Green fingers

If you have managed to get hold of some fresh herbs, once they have been washed and shaken dry, they will keep best chilled – either in a storage container or in a resealable freezer bag that you have blown air into.

Grilled fruit kebabs with spiced yogurt

For the yogurt

400g (14oz) full-fat yogurt
zest of 1 orange
1 tsp ground cardamom
½ tsp ground cinnamon
2 pinches of ground anise
pinch of ground cloves
20g (¾oz) chopped pistachios
1 tbsp sugar, plus extra to taste if needed

For the fruit kebabs

1 small pineapple, peeled, brown eyes
  removed, quartered lengthways, then cut
  into 4 equal-sized chunks
1 mango, flesh cut into bite-sized chunks
2 apricots, pitted, quartered, then each
  quarter halved
1 banana, cut into 3cm (1½in) thick slices

Also

4 wooden skewers (20cm/8in each)

1 Soak the wooden skewers for at least 30 minutes in water. To make the spiced yogurt, mix the yogurt with the orange zest, spices, pistachios, and sugar in a bowl, stirring until the sugar has dissolved. Add more sugar to taste, if desired.

2 To assemble the fruit kebabs, slide chunks of fruit alternately onto the skewers and grill on the barbecue over a low heat for 1 minute each side. Slide the fruit off the kebabs and divide between 4 plates. Serve with the spiced yogurt.

Chocolate cake baked in an orange

100g (3½oz) dark chocolate
1 tbsp cocoa powder
1 cup plain flour
1 tsp baking powder
salt
¾ cup icing sugar
4 oranges
2 tbsp soft butter
1 egg
2–3 drops vanilla extract

Also
8 pieces foil (30 × 30cm/12 x 12in each)

1 Finely grate the chocolate. This will be easier if you chill the chocolate for a while first. Combine the grated chocolate with the cocoa powder, flour, baking powder, a pinch of salt, and the icing sugar. The flour mixture can be prepared at home up to this point and stored in a container. The next steps can be continued at the campsite kitchen.

2 Slice a lid in the top quarter of the oranges. Hollow out the oranges with a spoon. Squeeze the pulp between your hands and measure out 175ml (6fl oz) orange juice. Put the flour mixture into a bowl or pan. Add the orange juice, butter, egg, and vanilla extract and stir with a wooden spoon until you have a smooth consistency.

3 Fill the hollowed-out oranges two-thirds full with the mixture and place the lids on to close. Wrap each one in 2 pieces of foil. Place on the barbecue and bake the cakes for about 30 minutes. Remove and leave to cool for 10 minutes then unwrap the foil and serve.

Campfire version
The oranges can be put directly into the embers of a campfire and cooked there. You may need to shorten or lengthen the cooking time, depending on how hot the embers are in the fire or on the barbecue. Ideally test the cakes with a skewer after about 20 minutes. If an inserted wooden skewer comes out with cake mixture on it, continue baking for another 5 minutes before testing again. The cake is cooked when the skewer comes out clean.

Ingredient packing list: Essential supplies

Which store-cupboard foods are absolutely essential for your travels? And what else could you pack if you have the room? Here is a list of travel basics and nice-to-have ingredients, which we suggest for making our recipes.

Basics

· maple syrup/honey
· baking powder
· Dijon/other mustard
· tinned tomatoes/passata/tomato purée
· vinegar
· drinks (water, lemonade, alcoholic beverages)
· instant stock powder or cubes
· coffee/tea
· garlic
· flour
· pasta
· oil
· pepper
· salt
· sugar
· onions

Nice to have

· couscous
· cocoa powder
· tins (such as beans, sweetcorn, and chickpeas)
· jam/chocolate hazelnut spread
· mie noodles
· nuts (including almonds) and seeds (such as sunflower seeds, cashews, and sesame seeds)
· icing sugar
· risotto rice
· soy sauce
· cornflour
· dried fruit (such as cranberries and apricots)
· dried yeast
· white breadcrumbs
· favourite spices and herbs (such as nutmeg, chilli powder, rosemary, oregano)

Equipment packing list that campers swear by

There are certain things nobody should be without in their mobile kitchen, such as a good knife, and then there are the luxury bits and bobs – the stuff you could do without but which make life just a little bit easier.

Basic kitchen equipment

- foil
- mugs/glasses/cups/plates (possibly camping crockery set)
- cutlery (knives, forks, tablespoons and teaspoons)
- freezer bags (resealable)
- tea towels
- wooden skewers
- wooden spoon
- corkscrew and tin opener
- kitchen paper
- measuring cup
- knives (2 x chef's knives, 2 x vegetable knives)
- rubbish bags
- frying pan (large, with lid)
- chopping board
- bowls (plus washing-up bowl if room)
- sieve
- potato peeler
- washing up liquid and sponges
- saucepans (no plastic handles, with lids)

Still got room to spare?

- espresso pot
- bamboo paddle skewers
- barbecue tongs
- garlic press
- kitchen twine
- spatula/fish slice
- grater (for vegetables and cheese)
- scissors
- balloon whisk
- silicone basting brush
- tablecloth

 Don't forget:
For the recipes you'll need a cup or your favourite camping mug with a capacity of 250ml (9fl oz) for measuring.

Index

A

apples
Apple and spinach salad with cranberry dressing **65**
Pan-cooked apple cake **110**
apricots
Apricot cakes in a jar **19**
Crispy baguette with turkey and apricots **36**
Instant couscous with apricots and macadamia nuts **90**
asparagus: Green asparagus salad with feta cheese **54**
aubergines
Greek pan-cooked pasta **80**
Pan-fried pork and beef with Mediterranean vegetables **133**
Stuffed steaks on a ratatouille and carrot base **117**
avocados: Orange and avocado salad with Dijon dressing **50**

B

bacon
Austrian omelette **76**
Bannock bread Alsace style **104**
Crispy baguette with turkey and apricots **36**
Ham and Cheddar wraps with honey-mustard sauce **44**
Hot dogs wrapped in bacon **125**
Pasta with cabbage and bacon **87**
bananas
Banana ketchup **15**
Grilled fruit kebabs with spiced yogurt **152**
Papaya, banana, and nut mix **32**
barbecues and grills **112–155**
beans and pulses
Barbecued balsamic bean parcels **143**
Green asparagus salad with feta cheese **54**
Sweet potato and pepper stew **95**
Tomato and sweetcorn salad with chickpeas **55**
beef
BBQ goulash **126**
Goulash with paprika and potatoes **73**
Pan-fried pork and beef with Mediterranean vegetables **133**
Pasta Bolognese alla Nonna **70**
Stuffed steaks on a ratatouille and carrot base **117**
Three tenderizing marinades **121**
breads
Bannock bread Alsace style **104**
Bread rolls from a pan **106**
Mini pan-cooked flatbreads **130**
Stick-bread options **135**
Stuffed flatbreads **109**
Broccoli salad with cashews and Roquefort dressing **53**

C

campfires **89, 134**
camping **8–9, 15, 88–89, 109**
equipment **10, 49, 66–67, 115, 157**
carrots
Chicken and vegetable mix with sautéed potatoes **92**
Grilled garden vegetables **142**
Stuffed steaks on a ratatouille and carrot base **117**
Vegetable stew with gnocchi **83**
cauliflower
Cauliflower cheese croquettes **84**
Cauliflower and courgette kebabs with almond salsa **140**
Salmon in foil with spiced cauliflower **147**
cheese
Antipasti veggie kebabs BBQ style **139**
Austrian omelette **76**
Barbecued herby Camembert **118**
BBQ pizza **136**
Broccoli salad with cashews and Roquefort dressing **53**
Cauliflower cheese croquettes **84**
Cheese and vegetable gnocchi **79**
Croque Madame 75
Fettuccine "Alfredo" **69**
Green asparagus salad with feta cheese **54**
Ham and Cheddar wraps with honey-mustard sauce **44**
Italian-style sandwiches with ricotta and ham **43**
Mini meatball skewers **26**
Potato gratin cooked on a camping BBQ **129**
Sandwiches with ricotta and figs **39**
Spiced nuts with pecorino **33**
Strawberry salad with mozzarella **56**
chicken
BBQ chicken in orange marinade **115**
Chicken and vegetable mix with sautéed potatoes **92**
Creamy instant noodles with mushrooms and pine nuts **91**
Instant curry rice with cashews **90**
Mexican instant rice with chicken **91**
Paella **99**

chocolate
Chocolate cake baked in an orange **155**
Strawberry sandwich **40**
courgettes
Antipasti veggie kebabs BBQ style **139**
Cauliflower and courgette kebabs with almond salsa **140**
couscous
Couscous salad with grapefruit dressing **59**
Instant couscous with apricots and macadamia nuts **90**
crackers
Poppy seed crackers with sesame **25**
Simple crackers **24**
cranberries
Apple and spinach salad with cranberry dressing **65**
Cranberry muesli bars **21**

E

eggs
Austrian omelette **76**
Croque Madame **75**
Spanish omelette **76**
Swedish omelette **77**

F

Fennel
Cod in a herby vegetable broth **103**
Orange and avocado salad with Dijon dressing **50**
fish & seafood
Barbecued sea bass **148**
Cod in a herby vegetable broth **103**
Mini sandwich rolls with creamed tuna **35**
see also mussels; prawns; salmon
food and drink
food for the journey **23–47**
foraging **88**
freeze-dried food **88, 90–91**
shelf life **48**
store cupboard items and recipes **12, 14–21, 48, 156**
storing food **48–49, 106, 129, 151**
water **13, 88**

G

gnocchi
Cheese and vegetable gnocchi **79**
Vegetable stew with gnocchi **83**
grapefruit

Couscous salad with grapefruit dressing **59**
Orange and avocado salad with Dijon
  dressing **50**
green beans
  BBQ goulash **126**
  Green asparagus salad with feta cheese **54**
  Grilled garden vegetables **142**

H
ham
  BBQ pizza **136**
  Croque Madame **75**
  Fettuccine "Alfredo" **69**
  Ham and Cheddar wraps with honey-mustard
    sauce **44**
  Italian-style sandwiches with ricotta and
    ham **43**
  Layered salad in a jar **29**
  Sandwiches with ricotta and figs **39**

K-L
kohlrabi
  Grilled garden vegetables **142**
  Vegetable stew with gnocchi **83**
leeks
  Mussels in white wine **100**
  Pan-fried sausage and leek with potatoes **74**

M
mangoes
  French toast with coconut and mango
    salad **111**
  Grilled fruit kebabs with spiced yogurt **152**
meat
  Mini meatball skewers **26**
  Spicy minced meat risotto **96**
  see also beef; chicken; pork; turkey
mushrooms
  Antipasti veggie kebabs BBQ style **139**
  Creamy instant noodles with mushrooms and
    pine nuts **91**
mussels
  Mussels in white wine **100**
  Paella **99**

N
nuts
  Broccoli salad with cashews and Roquefort
    dressing **53**
  Camping Bircher muesli mixture **20**
  Cauliflower and courgette kebabs with
    almond salsa **140**
  Cranberry muesli bars **21**
  Dukkah (spice mixture) **17**
  Honey-roasted peanuts **30**

Instant couscous with apricots and macadamia
  nuts **90**
Instant curry rice with cashews **90**
Papaya, banana, and nut mix **32**
Spiced nuts with pecorino **33**

O
oats
  Camping Bircher muesli mixture **20**
  Cranberry muesli bars **21**

P
Pancakes, eggless **47**
pasta and noodles
  Creamy instant noodles with mushrooms
    and pine nuts **91**
  Fettuccine "Alfredo" **69**
  Greek pan-cooked pasta **80**
  Pasta Bolognese alla Nonna **70**
  Pasta with cabbage and bacon **87**
peppers
  Antipasti veggie kebabs BBQ style **139**
  Barbecued balsamic bean parcels **143**
  BBQ chicken in orange marinade **115**
  BBQ sauce **16**
  Chicken and vegetable mix with sautéed
    potatoes **92**
  Goulash with paprika and potatoes **73**
  Spanish omelette **76**
  Sweet potato and pepper stew **95**
pineapple
  Grilled fruit kebabs with spiced yogurt **152**
  Hot dogs wrapped in bacon **125**
  Layered salad in a jar **29**
pork
  Goulash with paprika and potatoes **73**
  Pan-fried pork and beef with Mediterranean
    vegetables **133**
potatoes
  BBQ goulash **126**
  Chicken and vegetable mix with sautéed
    potatoes **92**
  Cod in a herby vegetable broth **103**
  Country potato salad **62**
  Goulash with paprika and potatoes **73**
  Grilled garden vegetables **142**
  Pan-fried sausage and leek with potatoes **74**
  Potato gratin cooked on a camping BBQ **129**
  Spanish omelette **76**
  Stuffed steaks on a ratatouille and carrot
    base **117**
prawns
  Paella **99**
  Prawn and lime kebabs **144**
  Swedish omelette **77**

R
radicchio
  Apple and spinach salad with cranberry
    dressing **65**
  Grilled radicchio salad **60**
Red onion confit **118**
rice
  Instant curry rice with cashews **90**
  Mexican instant rice with chicken **91**
  Paella **99**
  Spicy minced meat risotto **96**

S
salmon
  Lemony salmon with sesame seeds **151**
  Salmon in foil with spiced cauliflower **147**
sausages
  Grilled cherry tomato kebabs **123**
  Hot dogs wrapped in bacon **125**
  Pan-fried sausage and leek with potatoes **74**
  Spanish omelette **76**
  Stuffed flatbreads **109**
spinach
  Apple and spinach salad with cranberry
    dressing **65**
  Strawberry salad with mozzarella **56**
strawberries
  Strawberry salad with mozzarella **56**
  Strawberry sandwich **40**
Sweet potato and pepper stew **95**
sweetcorn
  Chicken and vegetable mix with sautéed
    potatoes **92**
  Grilled corn on the cob **122**
  Layered salad in a jar **29**
  Mexican instant rice with chicken **91**
  Tomato and sweetcorn salad with chickpeas **55**

T
tomatoes
  BBQ sauce **16**
  Grilled cherry tomato kebabs **123**
  Italian-style sandwiches with tahini and
    tomato **42**
  Ketchup **14**
  Mini meatball skewers **26**
  Pasta Bolognese alla Nonna **70**
  Salmon in foil with spiced cauliflower **147**
  Stuffed steaks on a ratatouille and carrot
    base **117**
  Tomato and sweetcorn salad with chickpeas **55**
turkey: Crispy baguette with turkey and
  apricots **36**

For DK UK

Translator Alison Tunley
Editor Claire Cross
Senior editor Kate Meeker
Editorial assistant Poppy Blakiston Houston
Senior art editor Glenda Fisher
Jacket designer Harriet Yeomans
Producer, pre-production Heather Blagden
Senior producer Igrain Roberts
Managing editor Stephanie Farrow
Managing art editor Christine Keilty

For DK Germany

Publisher Monika Schlitzer
Managing editor Caren Hummel
Project manager Anne Heinel, Melanie Haizmann
Production Dorothee Whittaker
Production coordinator Arnik a Marx
Producer Jenny Kolbe

First British Edition 2019
Dorling Kindersley Limited
80 Strand, London, WC2R 0RL

Copyright © 2018 Dorling Kindersley Verlag GmbH
Translation copyright © 2019 Dorling Kindersley Limited
Text copyright © 2018 Viola Lex, Nico Stanitzok
Photography copyright © 2018 Brigitte Sporrer/DK Verlag
A Penguin Random House Company
10 9 8 7 6 5 4 3 2 1
001–314121–April/2019

A CIP catalogue record for this book
is available from the British Library.
ISBN: 978-0-2413-7773-4

Printed and bound in China

A WORLD OF IDEAS:
SEE ALL THERE IS TO KNOW

www.dk.com

Survival stuff for campers

We've given you plenty of advice and information about the campsite kitchen, but we couldn't send you off on your travels without a few more suggestions for everyday kit. Before starting your camping trip, remember the following:

Essentials

- cash (in the relevant national currency); debit and/or credit card
- bed linen; sleeping mat; air bed; sleeping bag
- glasses; contact lenses + solution
- lighter and/or matches
- vehicle registration document; driving licence (international); vehicle hire documents, if relevant
- passport, if needed
- torch and/or headlamp

Clothes and accessories

- flip flops for the showers
- suitable and sufficient clothes for the weather, length of trip, and luggage restrictions
- cool box and batteries
- sunglasses
- a rucksack for day trips